Connecting to your
'universal piggy bank'

'Wealth workout' techniques to help you make more money and achieve your wants, dreams and desires.

Madison King

CONTENTS

INTRODUCTION

THIS BOOK COULD CHANGE YOUR LIFE !

If you are reading this now the chances are you WANT something and you're not getting it.

- What is blocking you?
- What is tripping you up?
- What is sabotaging you?
- What is stopping you?
- What is the hurdle you can't jump over?

Whatever it is, it will have an 'energetic' dimension to it and the good news is that energy can be moved.

I have always believed that there is a form of divine timing in everything and that something 'looks after' me, and I still do. I have also come to the conclusion that by working with my energies I can profoundly influence my life; how I live it and the degree to which I enjoy it. I love connecting with my kind, nurturing and generous 'Universal Piggy Bank'.

It wasn't always that way and when I look back I smile and cringe in equal measure at how lonely I felt. From an early age I was convinced I had to look after myself, nobody else did, or would. I stumbled through my early life, parenting and supporting myself. My struggle was, in the end, successful, but with hindsight I feel life could have been far less angst ridden, if only I had known about my Universal Piggy Bank – how much easier and happier life might have been! But enough of roaming around the kingdom of 'what if's' – the reality

1

is I've found him now, am connecting to him, building my relationship with him and totally trust that he will somehow find the ways of manifesting what I want, in the most inventive and divine way. It doesn't necessarily mean I can just sit back and do absolutely nothing but between us we can make magic.

If you wonder what I mean by my 'Universal Piggy Bank' – it is my pet name for a universal 'energy' that each of us can tap into for support and abundance. I don't pretend to be able to define it exactly or scientifically, but it exists and if you can tap into it, life definitely begins to flow with more ease.

Entering my seventh decade I am happier than I have ever been before; abundant and rich in all the things I hold dear. People have asked me for 'my secret' so I decided to share with you, some of the things that have worked for me personally and that I have taught students over the years.

First of all, I want to encourage you not to live life constantly looking through your rear view mirrors, it doesn't really gain you anything, in fact it could cause havoc in your life. Don't use your past as a convenient hook upon which to hang the disappointments of the present. Learn from it and move on. Where you are now is a fact, it's a reality whether you like it or not. You can't change the past but you can enjoy the present and look forward, with a smile, to the future with your Universal Piggy Bank [UPB].

Let's be realistic, no one 'way' will work for everyone all the time – but if you were drawn to this book, if it has appeared in your life, it is probably the right thing for you at this moment and will help you get 'unstuck', move the energies in your life and help turn your dreams, desires and 'wants' into reality.

The energy techniques I am going to share with you will help _you_ 'get what you want' in, and out, of _your_ life.

Let's start off by being honest and owning up to the fact that at the root of a lot of our 'wants' is the need for good old 'dosh', 'ackers', a bit of 'ready', dough, moolah, spondulicks – in other words: money! It can, in many instances, provide a hyperlink to your 'want'.

Money can buy you a car, travel, clothes, healthcare, good food, safe shelter and little books like this. It can enable you to help your loved ones and any charity you choose, it can build hospitals, it can provide education. Money is NOT the root of all evil as our grannies loved telling us. This sort of dogmatic belief inhibits our freedom to change the paradigm of our personal lives and build a healthy relationship with money.

Let's also knock on the head the whole misconception that you are selfish if you put yourself first; if you _want_ money. There is no currency whatsoever in being a martyr, it benefits nobody and nothing. If you can gain health and wealth you are in a far better position to help others. I was listening to an interview with Suze

Orman[1] the other day and she highlighted the analogy of the oxygen mask on a plane: you put your mask on before you help the children or others – sort *yourself* out first then you are in a position to help those around you.

- How comfortable are you with simply saying, slowly and deliberately: "I want money"?

- Is your relationship with money comfortable?

- Do you believe you are a better person if you are not interested in money and don't talk about it?

- Do you think talking about money is vulgar?

It is what we do with the money, not the money itself that is good, bad, ugly or indifferent. Greed, avarice, destructive competitiveness and fear of loss carry a highly charged negative energy; that £20 note in your wallet doesn't!

MONEY can be the root of an awful lot of good in this world – for ourselves and others.

How we feel about money can be a reflection of how we feel about ourselves. The two are intricately linked, so take a moment to reflect, could there be something that money is trying to tell you? If your finances are unhealthy, are you?

---

1 www.suzeorman.com

What we 'do' with our lives is a real barometer to our happiness – we spend so much time working – are you HAPPY in your work? It would be Pollyanna to suggest that we should all be ecstatic every morning on the way to work but at the very least we should not be in the depths of despair at the thought of facing another week doing what we do. I was watching a documentary on Richard Branson the other day and it struck me how much 'fun' he had in building his business empire: there were successes and failures but he laughed a lot and obviously enjoyed it all... and boy he really did connect to his Universal Piggy Bank !

It is a truly rich person that enjoys their work, and because they enjoy it they very often do it extremely well – do you need a change?

Four times I have 'chucked it all in' and totally changed my life in the pursuit of happiness rather than just plain money:

- From student to Euro-hippy [can't remember much about that!]
- Euro-hippy to mainstream London advertising director [of course with the obligatory 80's shoulder pads, BMW and Gucci briefcase]
- Director to student again, this time of many natural healthcare fields and of course; Eden Energy Medicine. Was blessed with the most amazing teachers in each field I choose to study
- From successful Central London Energy Practitioner to living half way up a hillside in Andalucía! So much for retirement, I'm busier

than ever with my teaching, writing, online study groups and setting up EEM[2] in Europe

Okay, so I'm an abundant and rich woman...

You may be sitting there asking: well, if she knows all this stuff, why isn't she an actual millionaire yet?! Well, because that is not what I have called in, it's not what I have asked for: I have worked with dozens of millionaires [and the odd billionaire] and am aware that such wealth has its own set of problems that I don't particularly want to deal with.

What I call in is: I don't have a heart attack every time a bill drops on my mat, if my car suddenly needs new tyres or repairs I don't panic and I very rarely have to say 'no' to myself – if I *really* want to buy something I usually do, although I have to admit my needs have become far more modest these days. If I need money to meet an unexpected and large bill, my Universal Piggy Bank always manages to deliver.

My wants are what make ME happy, not someone else, not you; they are my own personal desires and ambitions and have been fine tuned over six decades. No longer heavily influenced by clever marketing and advertising, they probably won't suit everyone but they definitely suit me. I seek peace not adrenalin churning excitement [had enough of that thank you]; gentle anonymity rather than any type of fame, supporting students and helping them, the next generation, grow rather than taking

---

2 Eden Energy Medicine – developed by Donna Eden in USA www.innersource.net

centre stage myself... although I am sure in a past life I was an actress as I love strutting around teaching! Walking the dogs on the beach at sunrise brings me more joy than roaring down the motorway in the latest Ferrari, not that I wouldn't enjoy that too but it is not high on my list of priorities.

Being able to take two months off work to walk the Camino de Santiago [a long held dream] makes me feel blessed and very very lucky and 'rich'.

Being able to buy organic vegetables from a local grower or exploring Harrods Food Hall where they have a few good things to tempt a girl! Have you seen their Belgium chocolates recently? You get the idea.

I consider myself a 'rich' woman; wealthy and abundant in all the things I have come to hold precious in my life. Money is all about enabling you to do what makes YOU happy – so I'm off down the beach now, to walk the dogs!

I love the security and therefore freedom I am gaining in slowly letting go of my fear of loss and dread of poverty, of endless anxiety of what 'might' happen. Instead, I'm beginning to trust that what I need will come in – albeit sometimes in its own time. It enables me to sleep at night and not worry over every single bill that drops on my mat. It means I feel safe to take the time [and money] for self care and some great treats now and again. I'm not perfect, I still have the odd 'wobble', of course I do – but I'm getting there and I want to help you get there too.

I want to help you love money, embrace it, have a healthy relationship with it, have fun with it and not turn your back on it.

Action conquers fear and I want to help you take action and responsibility for your wealth and manifestation of your wants ... deep down inside you know that you are the *only* person who is really interested and who can do something. The whole point of this book is to give you the tools to do that 'something'.

They say [and science is proving] that everything is energy;
so it therefore follows that money is too!
One of the fundamental concepts of energy medicine is about moving and balancing the flow of energy.
These same principles apply
to the energy of money.
You can move it... and move it in your direction.

Take a while to decide and define what it is you want and follow my strategy to make it happen – do it with lightness, fun and an open mind. After all, we get what we expect so expect the very best!

From this moment on don't doubt.
Still that little chattering voice nagging away at
you.

The Universal Piggy Bank invariably does provide what we need, often with great grace; you can make her job a whole lot easier by telling her clearly what it is you want.

'Wants' can be physical, emotional or spiritual and very often our efforts to fulfil them are thwarted by a distinct lack of 'cash flow'. Money doesn't buy happiness but it does buy good quality food, clothes, comfortable shelter, travel, music even my books and workshops and perhaps most important of all, it can buy you time to smell the roses and enjoy any of the above. Many good things in life are free, but an awful lot depend upon having the cash to help bridge the gap between 'wanting' and 'achieving'.

When your energy system stops worrying then so do you!

If you are not constantly anxious about how to pay the bills, your Triple Warmer[3] and root chakra[4] begin to relax; your survival needs are being met. You will free up vital energy that can be used for other things in life, from healing yourself, helping others, to spiritual reflection or to simply having more fun and time out; to start living the life you want to live.

---

3 A pathway of energy that responds directly to any stress or perceived threat to your survival.

4 This chakra is associated with survival issues, of which money is one.

Energy medicine can not only create health in your body but also a *healthy wealthy wallet* and can be an invaluable tool in helping you get what you want.

You can work at whatever 'depth' you choose. There is a simple 'fix it all' technique that works for a lot of people with a damaged core belief around money. If self esteem and 'safety' are issues for you, head for Part Two once you have fixed your core belief. There is also a more detailed and complex technique that addresses possible fears that are blocking you achieving your 'wants'. Work at the level that suits you.

- It is *not* about acquiring great piles of money and sitting like Scrooge counting it up.
- It is never about building your fortune to the detriment of others.
- It is about always having enough to meet your needs, about trusting the flow, in and out, the energy 'breath' of money. The wave of wealth.
- It is about sharing what you have with others.

I would also like to address the whole question of timing [always divine] – it can be frustrating that the UPB[5] sometimes dances to a different beat – but trust in the timing, it will be divine and it will be right.

I began to doubt, just a little, when I was selling my house in London – boy, it took a long time and I was doing everything I knew. However, with hindsight I recognise that the timing was indeed superb, it couldn't have been

5 UPB – to avoid always having to read the full Universal Piggy Bank

more perfect – everything, absolutely everything fell into place all of a sudden and it all felt so darn 'right'! So, don't be despondent, keep the faith and trust the timing of the UPB!

That's what I've got to say; let's see what other people have said about want, wealth and money:

*"Gratitude for the present moment and
the fullness of life now is true prosperity."*
Eckart Tolle

*"It is not the creation of wealth that is wrong,
but the love of money for its own sake."*
Margaret Thatcher

*"Money is better than poverty, if only for financial
reasons."*
Woody Allen

*"It's a kind of spiritual snobbery that
makes people think they can be happy without money."*
Albert Camus

*"There are people who have money and people who are
rich."*
Coco Chanel

*"Money is only a tool. It will take you wherever you
wish, but it will not replace you as the driver."*
Ayn Rand

"Do what you love and the money will follow."
Marsha Sinetar

"True Persons do not hoard.
Using all they have for others, they still have more.
Giving all they have to others, they are richer than
before."
Lao Tzu

"Money isn't the most important thing in life,
but it's reasonably close to oxygen on
the "gotta have it" scale."
Zig Ziglar

"What we really want to do is what we are really
meant to do. When we do what we are meant to do,
money comes to us, doors open for us, we feel useful,
and the work we do feels like play to us."
Julia Cameron

"Money is kind of a base subject. Like water, food, air
and housing, it affects everything yet for some reason
the world of academics thinks it's a
subject below their social standing."
Robert Kiyosaki

"Abundance is not something we acquire.
It is something we tune into."
Wayne Dyer

Money can't buy you happiness... but it does bring you
a more pleasant form of misery!
Spike Milligan
[I love this one]

Don't they get you thinking? There are some great books, dvds and workshops out there on this theme, take a look around, visit You Tube to hear some inspiration speakers. See what feels right for you, what inspires, motivates and most of all, be objective and see what **works** for you. This is what works for me and I suspect it will help you too.

Don't fall for the argument that money is the root of all evil or it lowers your 'spiritual vibration' and that poverty is noble: why? Again, it's what you do to get the money and then how you use it that can be evil.

Money itself replaced bartering as a convenient and practical way to exchange goods and services – it wouldn't really be feasible nowadays to walk around with a couple of chickens and some runner beans in your bag to 'buy' your loaf of bread and pound of fish; far easier to carry a few coins and notes. Money is just paper, metal and, with online banking, simply 'stuff' on the airwaves – it is what we do with it that makes it noble or ignoble.

You should always behave with 100% honour, honesty, fairness, kindness, compassion and integrity. Make a commitment, an agreement with yourself, right now, to do so; to treat others as you would wish to be treated. You'll find it has a boomerang effect, it bounces back to you. If we all lived by this code what a wonderful world it would be.

Is money a practical 'tool' in your personal life or has it become your own personal God? It should be able to achieve things for yourself and those around you with an incredible lightness of being – it should make a real difference, it should be loved and enjoyed but it should never ever be blindly worshipped.

The core of this work is aligning the energy of each meridian [pathway of energy] with the energy of money. This ensures that the meridian is strengthened by that energy and not weakened.

Once your energies no longer feel threatened by money they begin to embrace it, resonate with it and attract it to them. That's the secret.

Out of the different energy systems I have chosen meridians because they are like the 'lavender' of energy – gentle yet effective and they affect every nook and cranny of your body. They are the bridge between mind body and spirit. However, the technique will work very well with the Strangeflows [also called Radiant Circuits or Extraordinary vessels] or chakras: adapt it to what feels right for you if you know energies. If it is all new to you just follow my basic instructions.

It doesn't take long to change an energetic habit and then just a bit of discipline to make sure you don't fall back into that 'bad' habit. You will find that the investment you make in time and effort will be repaid tenfold. So read through, decide what you want and what approach you are going to take – plan it and then do it. It won't work unless you do it, so get started – NOW.

Madison x

Southern Spain June 2013

PART ONE
ALL ABOUT MONEY

Everyone will benefit from
doing the work in this section

Help in defining what you actually want in life

What do YOU really want? Not what your parents, husband, children, friends, peers, society, government or advertising and marketing departments tell you you should want.

Your first step is to challenge yourself, '*I want to be happy*' is something we would all aspire to but take it further, WHAT is going to make you happy? '*I want to be healthier*' again, scrape away at that statement, WHAT would help you become healthier? Better food? More exercise? More discipline? More ability to make the right choices on both? True happiness some say, is the art of finding happiness in the present moment, however elusive it may seem.

Be focussed, realistic and as uncomplicated as possible. Treat yourself to some time out to decide. It's in the quiet time when the mind stops its bleating that you can truly connect with the truth inside you.

There may be several things you want – take time to consider and define your priority at *this* point in time.

- I want to change my job and do something I really enjoy.
- I want to be an actress/doctor/reflexologist/EEM practitioner

- I want to work less and earn more
- I want to work less and keep a great standard of living
- I want to feel good about wanting/receiving money
- I want more time for myself and not have to work so much
- I want to get out of debt
- I want to have £X amount in my bank account by this time next year [write a cheque to yourself for the amount and pin it on your fridge or notice board – sign it The Universal Banker]
- I want to leave this destructive relationship
- I want to mend my broken heart
- I want a loving relationship – on or before [choose a realistic date just a few months from now]
- I want to feel safe, loved and cared for
- I want to sell my house
- I want a new car
- I want to walk the Camino
- I want to swim with dolphins in Mexico
- I want to live in the South of France
- I want to be an artist/write a book/climb that mountain
- I want to travel
- I want to be slim
- I want to get fit
- I want to be healthy

It is essential that the 'want' is simple, focussed and clear. Don't get complicated or overanalyse; this can result in confusion rather than clarity... if you are confused, the energy around your 'want' becomes clouded, flow is diminished and results are not forthcoming. Clarity is your chum.

Sometimes we get so stressed with everyday life and its demands we don't actually know or articulate what it is we want.

Clear the energetic stress cobwebs to find that quiet place within, so that you can at least hear what the wise woman inside has to say. Listen to the whispers of your 'inner sage'.

Breathing is a quick and effective way to do this, it is like sending a text to your nervous system with a message to relax.

One simple breathing exercise I do is:

Sit or lie down – get comfortable and bring your attention to your breathing, don't try and control it, just observe and try smiling while you breathe, I heard somewhere you oxygenate more effectively when you smile and breath at the same time.

INHALE to the count of ten

HOLD the breath to the count of ten

EXHALE to the count of fifteen

[you can change the count – always make the exhale longer]

Hold your hands in this mudra – Metal Element – connecting Large Intestine and Lung meridians – great for letting go of all the excess stress, anxiety and mental 'chattering' that can obscure our true 'wants'. The forefinger represents Large Intestine and the thumb Lung. You can either put the two pads together or thumb pad over index fingernail.

An alternative is to sit at your table, rest your forehead on your middle fingers [so they are resting on the neurovascular stress points located in line with your pupils half way between your eyebrow and hairline] index and thumb still in mudra and should fall naturally on the triple warmer points located on both temples. Do the breathing while in this position. You may want to repeat the affirmation:

'I am now stress free and can see clearly what I really want in life'.

THE GENIE IN YOUR HAND

The eighth point on your heart meridian [on either hand] is a perfect point to massage/rub hard while you ponder upon what you want, it is said to bring clarity and reveal your heart's desire.

The 8th point is easily located if you put your hand in a fist and where the little finger lands is the point.

Start living your life by doing

what makes you happy.

Define what

you need to do to make you happy,

identify what is missing.

"Change your mind - change your life"

Was originally quoted by Louise Hay[6] and is wise indeed.

---

6 www.louisehay.com

The more you do this simple process, the more you reconnect with what you really want in life and the less you are influenced by the conditioning of your past, of society and of marketing. Plug into your real dreams, regain the energy to manifest them and enjoy living them. Do what makes you happy.

This is not just hedonism, living a life wealthy in good things, frees our energy from being totally tied up in pure survival. It frees us to pursue our spiritual path, to raise our awareness and share our abundance.

Think back to school and Maslow's Hierarchy of Needs [1943]. If all your time is taken up with providing for food, drink and shelter; there is very little time or energy left for your relationships and also for working and developing yourself, achieving your full potential and consciously walking your spiritual path.

Let's be frank, if the basics of life are taken care of with money; nutritious food, plentiful water, warm, dry and safe shelter – if you have enough of that it gives you good firm roots upon which to climb the pyramid, to live the life you were born to live.

So, deal with your basic needs first – ask for money to help you. It could be as simple as: *I want enough money to pay my rent and bills with no worries.*

As Donna Eden says: '*Energy really is all there is*'. Money is just energy and we can work with energy, we can encourage it to flow; we can encourage a healthy flow of money in our life.

If your view of money has become distorted it will block your ability to attract it. Fall in love with money; recognise it for what it is; merely a tool that can be used for ultimate good. It is not greedy to want money, so long as you don't hurt anyone getting it and then try and hang on to it, that fear of losing it is what can cause problems. Focus on the flow: it will come into your life and out, in again and out – like eternal waves of abundance.

Our fear urges us to squirrel away, hoard and save our money [nothing wrong with saving, in fact saving is essential sometimes – but as in all things in life, there is a balance, a healthy moderation]. Worldwide savings amount to about 70 trillion dollars ! There about 7 billion people on the planet – now doesn't that put a different perspective on it for you. There are literally trillions of dollars swirling around the world right now. Clear your blocks and get a bigger slice of the universal pie.

We all desire to feel safe, loved, cared for and money can help us meet these basic survival needs. Although if you take time to ponder upon your life at the moment you are probably: safe, rich, wealthy and cared for – the majority of us are but it is how we perceive our lives that creates our 'reality'.

If you feel damaged by disappointment – work on it, don't be diminished by it – cultivate your ability to respond and move on.

Our needs are clearly represented in Abraham Maslow's hierarchy of needs

Starting with the basics:

PHYSIOLOGICAL – breathing, food, water, shelter, clothing, sleep, sex, excretion.

SAFETY – security of body, employment, resources, morality, the family, health and property.

LOVE/BELONGING – friendship, family, sexual intimacy and a sense of connection.

ESTEEM – self esteem, confidence, achievement, respect of others, respect by others. Your own special uniqueness and individuality: finding it and honouring it.

SELF ACTUALISATION – morality, creativity, spontaneity, problem solving, lack of prejudice, acceptance of facts; gaining meaning and awareness of spiritual journey.

If you raise the vibration around money issues in your life, you raise the energy and enable movement 'up' Maslow's pyramid. Turn the fear and restriction of the lower levels to the freedom of the higher levels. Evolve. We weave up and down depending upon circumstances but ideally we need to be operating from the top of the pyramid for the majority of the time. Our basic levels are being threatened on a global level at the moment. If 'they' keep us busy here they slow our rise up the pyramid and our ability to question how the world is run.

self
actualise

Self esteem,
confidence, respect
and integrity.

Love, belonging, friendship,
family, sense of connection.

Safety and security: health, employment
property, family and social stability.

Pure survival needs: breathing, food, water, shelter, clothing
and sleep. We cannot rise up the pyramid until these are
taken care of.

With the reality of the world we live in, we may move between the different sections as each requires our attention at particular times but ultimately we should be operating primarily from the top.

In this way we evolve and are able to help others evolve too.

Maslow's pyramid could be likened to the Chakra system – every section is valid and needs to be balanced and fulfilled. They form a team intent on your wellbeing.

WHAT IS YOUR CORE BELIEF?
Test it and find out.

Before we go any further; I've been rattling on about our attitude to money. Let's test to see what your 'core' belief is. Intellectually you may have been nodding your head as you read, but what does that area beyond your conscious intellect feel? What is its true belief about money? What do the very cells in your body feel about money? Metaphorically speaking that is.

What do I mean by 'testing'? I want to share with you one of the basic and most valuable tools of energy medicine – the simple energy test.

First, let's look at testing another person. It's very easy, so just relax and enjoy it. As stress of any kind inhibits energy flow, the more relaxed you are the more accurate the test will be.

Your friend stands up straight and relaxed, with feet apart. [If necessary, the test can be done sitting].

If you go on my site www.midlifegoddess.ning.com [7]and click on the videos section there are a couple of clips of me demonstrating the energy test. Sometimes it is easier to see it rather than read it. Especially if you have never come across testing before.

Left arm [or right] is held out at a right angle to the body and parallel to the floor – this isolates the muscle that we want to test. [see position in photo].

Check hand is *not* clenched into a fist – fingers should be straight.

Stand in front of your friend, not too close, with your right hand, palm flat and facing downwards

---

7 Being a woman, in fact being a Midlife Goddess, I have used the feminine throughout this book, with no intentional slight to any wonderful Midlife God that might be reading the pages.

and fingers extended – resting on your friend's raised arm, on the forearm near the wrist joint. [shoulder side of the wrist].

The left hand can rest gently on her shoulder.

Demonstrate the range of movement [from that position down to the side of the body] – so that she is confident in what is about to happen. *You are interested in the first couple of inches* of that range, not everyone's arm drops all the way down to their hip. It might be that a 'spongy' response is all that is felt, but that is enough to indicate a weak result.

Tell her to 'HOLD' – wait half a second, while her brain registers the command and then apply pressure for 2 seconds maximum – gently, no jerking movements.

What happened? If it stays in position easily it means that it is testing STRONG, the person is 'generally' strong.

However, if it is spongy, or falls all the way down then that is a WEAK test. The person is 'generally' weak.

If it is the first time testing, it is a good idea to check that the person is testing correctly.

You do this by the following procedure:

Deliberately weaken the person by running the palm of your hand backwards along the Central meridian[8] [i.e. **down** the centre of their torso] this takes a couple of seconds.

TEST

– it should be weak i.e. the arm will go down or be spongy.

Now run your palm up along the flow of Central

[**up** the centre of the torso].

TEST

– it should be strong.

This gives you a feel of their individual range and confirms they are testing correctly. That is you can get a strong result and a weak result.

TESTING YOUR CORE BELIEF ABOUT MONEY

Now say the first statement [Money is a good, positive thing] and energy test.

---

8 Tracing backwards on any channel of energy will weaken the body. Central meridian runs up the body, so tracing down the body is against the flow and will weaken the person. At the end of the test, always ensure you trace upwards to leave the person strong.

Are you strong?

If so then you may not have a negative belief about
money.

Are you weak?

It may be that there is a negative belief that you
need to work on before the energy of money can
truly flow in your life.

Testing the quadriceps muscle is an
easy and reliable self test:

Sit straight on a chair, with feet
firmly planted on the ground in
front, the chair should neither be
too high nor too low.

Lift one leg slightly off the chair. Now,
with the heel of your hand, press down
on that knee, while the knee resists.

If the leg stays locked take it as a strong result but if the
leg goes down easily then it is a weak result.

> Money is a good, positive thing

> Money is a bad, negative thing

Energy test each statement.

Either get someone else to test you or test yourself.

Did the results surprise you?

> *Do the same test against your 'want'*
> *and note the results. We'll come back to it later.*

At this point we are focussing on the biggest stumbling block to achieving your 'want' – in more than 85% of cases the hurdle you have to jump is a 'money' one. So, if your 'want' tests weak now, retest after you have done the money technique and it will probably test strong. You will have removed the biggest barrier to achieving your desire.

The energy of money is not about greed, it is about loving life and others, about sharing your wealth and evolving.

It is about flow not hoarding.

Money is no guarantee whatsoever against suffering or the lessons in life that present themselves as challenges; it may be one of those lessons needs you to suffer poverty to learn from it but not necessarily, the chances are you have a choice!

Before we go any further let's get comfortable with the energy of money, let's break through some of those conditionings that hold us back from getting what we want. At the very least let's get your basic survival needs met.

If you tested weak against the money statement – there is a generalised 'weakness' around the money issue. Let's test to see, in more depth, what specific energies your money belief is weakening by testing it against key meridians [energy pathways in the body]. If we know this we can correct it more effectively.

I would suggest that even if you tested strong on the general test, that you do the following one, just to make sure nothing has slipped under the radar to sabotage you. We are working with the subconscious [I call it Mini-me] and it can be very cunning in putting you off the scent so to speak. If money is not as abundant and forthcoming as you would like it to be, or need it to be; the chances are that there will be some sort of weakness in the energies – it only takes a minute so out smart Mini-me and test each meridian.

TESTING 'MONEY' AGAINST EACH MERIDIAN and their meanings

Each pathway of energy has its own unique character, while still being part of the whole, a member of the pack, it is also highly individual. Which one is affected/weakened by the 'money' issue, gives you a clue as to the underlying emotion behind it.

The simplest way to test each meridian is to hold a coin or the highest denomination note that you have in your wallet, against one of the meridian's end points [there are two on each meridian, select the easiest to locate and work with]: focus on it, bring your attention to it, saying the name of the meridian and the word *'money'* out loud if that helps bring focus and then test it. Points are on both sides of the body [except for Central and Governing] – test them all.

If you don't have a coin then simply hold the meridian ending and say a money statement such as:

'I love money and money loves me'
or
'money is a good a positive thing and I want lots'

I tend to use cash rather than a credit card for this particular test as a credit card can carry the energy or association of 'debt' which is another matter. Cash is a purer representative of money.

Copy the chart below and record your results.

Energy pathway	Associated emotion	Location to test	L	R
Central	*Vulnerability*	Cleft in chin		
Governing	*Courage/ backbone*	Cupids bow on upper lip		
Stomach	*Obsessive worry*	Just under eye		
Spleen	*Anxiety/others*	Under arm where bra sits [monkey thump]		
Heart	*Self love/ esteem*	Pad of little finger		
Small Intestine	*Feeling divided*	Finger nail of little finger		
Bladder	*futility*	The inside of the eye		
Kidney	*Fear New beginnings*	K27 points in the junction between collar bones and breastbone		
Circ Sex	*Panic*	Just on the outside of your nipples		
Triple Warmer	*stress*	Hold the end of the ring finger		
Gallbladder	*Outwardly directed anger*	temples		
Liver	*Inwardly directed anger*	Big toe nail on inside edge next to 2nd toe		
Lung	*Grief*	thumb		
Large Intestine	*Holding on*	Index finger		

What could a weakness in a specific meridian mean?

We are not examining a weakness in any great depth: but it is nevertheless interesting and sometimes revealing to know what emotions are associated with your money issue.

However, don't get too sidetracked by it, working with the energy will help resolve the imbalance. Over analysing can cause even more stress around it, unless you are with a trained practitioner who can effectively guide you through the minefield of 'why'.

Central	Is all about vulnerability. How we relate to, or hook up to, others and our environment. It is about feeling centred, secure and strong; about respect and success. About feeling confident to meet the challenge in front of you.
	You need to be careful that you are not acting as a 'sponge' and taking on everyone else's problems, or at least the energy of those problems. If that happens it can prevent you moving on in your own life.
	Zip up [see exercises] repeating the statement: "I am clear, centred, secure and confident that I am getting what I want – quickly and easily, all is well".

Governing	The name of the game for Governing is: Courage, backbone and the ability to move forward. We sometimes need courage to take a risk to get where we want to be and achieve our 'want'. [Note that taking an informed risk/ investment, is very different from chance/gambling]. Ensuring Governing is in harmony, provides you with a sense of a strong hand pushing you forward, of clarity and lack of confusion, of standing tall and being truly in your power – "YES! I can do this, and I can do it well!!"
Stomach	Obsessive worry. Feeling insecure. Value yourself or you will be undervalued. Trust the process, trust that when you launch yourself off the cliff you will sprout your wings and fly on the way down. Stomach is the home of truly trusting the Universe; of not resisting but surrendering. It is where we learn to put ourselves top on our priority list and not feeling 'bad' or 'selfish' about admitting that we 'want' something. Stomach sits in Earth element, it is important to get it strong so that you can root, ground, earth you and your projects. Were your 'roots' damaged as a child? Is that impacting on your decisions and life now? Learn to trust in the mystery of life, let go of unnecessary anxiety, relax and enjoy the ride. You can't change the past so ground in the present and be confident about the future.

Spleen	Home of anxiety.
	Also the home of transformation.
	You really benefit from a strong Spleen when you are working on your wants.
	Spleen energy will help you process the change with ease.
	It is the root of post heaven energy [i.e. the energy produced by the body after birth] – it gives vitality to your wants.
	You can give out 100% and work hard in the pursuit of your 'want' but you also need to ensure that you learn the gentle art of replenishment.
Heart	Self love/esteem.
	Learn to love yourself; madly, deeply and completely!
	Is your 'want' emanating from your heart or your head?
	Live with integrity; listen to the wisdom of the heart.
	It's about loving life, people and self and being in the present moment and enjoying it.
	It is about heartfelt gratitude and embracing life.
	When you are with someone, learn to really listen to them, listen with your heart – this is true emotional giving.

Small Intestine	Decisions and discernment, two powerful allies. Feeling divided. Gutsy transformations come from a strong Small Intestine. It is the seat of discernment, of accessing the wisdom of our intuitive self to discover what is essential and true and what is not. In today's world, we have to make more and more choices; some of them profoundly affecting and transforming our lives: choosing a partner, job, place to live etc., we need to make 'wise' choices. Small intestine is about sorting through what we want and what we don't want resulting in clarity. If we don't have this we operate from a confused and indecisive state.
Bladder	Home of Hope – is how I think of Bladder. Sometimes we sink into futility, where it all seems so useless and pointless. We get caught up on this merry go round and can't get off. We are fearful and that fear can often stand between you and your 'want'.

Kidney	Let go of the fear of losing it all, then you don't hold on to it, you let it flow and that my friend, is true freedom. What is the point of wealth if you become scared of it or of being without it? Relax around money, move from ego conditioning to energy/spiritual perspective. There is a story I've heard about Stuart Wilde, carrying around £2,000 and leaving bits of it in different places, not buying anything, just leaving it. As a true statement to the Universe that there is no fear in letting it go, only the unshakable belief that it will return... Kidney is where it all begins. The very first meridian, the source of energy for the entire system. Kidney is about new beginnings. Ensure it is strong, so you have plenty of 'juice' to get what you want and to transform that fear and doubt into wisdom and trust.
Circ Sex	Panic, bewilderment and neglecting your hearts needs. This meridian is also called Heart Protector as it does just that. We have a need for a strong yet flexible protector and if we have that, we can bravely face anything that life springs on us. We don't need to avoid anything in life for fear of being 'hurt'; we can therefore live life more easily and to the absolute full.

Triple Warmer	All about safety – and we each want to feel safe. It is also about stress and we could all do with less of that. Calm it down and calm down the stress response in the body which in turn allows energy to flow more freely – and money is energy! It is also a 'radiant circuit' and has the remarkable characteristic, when in balance of bringing joy into our lives and attracting change. An absolute 'must' in bringing your want into the realms of reality. Let go of competing, there is no need. If your peers, colleagues, friends need the ego satisfaction of being the 'big shots' being right all the time – let them. Start acting and living simply, being more at peace – it raises your energy and helps raise the money energy too.
Gallbladder	*Outwardly* directed anger. Anger is natural; feel it and let it pass through and out of you. It can get in the way of achieving your wants. Gallbladder is about vision, beliefs; about decisions and determination – all essential in materialising your wants. The Japanese believe that Gallbladder energy influences courage and initiative and provides guts and go ahead.

Liver	*Inwardly* directed anger. Stop it right now if you are angry at yourself. Let it go and move on.
	Liver is like an Army General, with a strong Liver energy you can assess your situation, conceive plans and strategies to get what you want.
	This is the 'mover and shaker', the 'do-er' of the meridian system. Get him on side, quickly.
	You can't win the lottery unless you buy a ticket! Action moves possibilities into realities. Every day take at least ONE action that will contribute to successfully getting what you want – go buy that lottery ticket.
Lung	Grief may be holding you back. You may be storing grief from decades ago that was not expressed. Work on releasing grief, exhaling it and inhaling fresh, new, clean air into your life.
	When you breathe out you have the ultimate, unshakeable belief that there will be air to breathe in. You need to develop this sort of belief and harness it to your wants. They will really take off if you can do this. Develop TOTAL TRUST.

Large Intestine	Holding on. Start letting go of all that old emotional baggage that is holding you back, toxic thoughts and physical clutter in your car, office or home. Cut the guy ropes and watch yourself soar as you achieve your wants.
	Clutter clear – give stuff away to kick start the flow of £ energy and to create space for good things to come into your life.
	Giving means someone feels joy of receiving. Generosity though is not just with cash and 'things' but also with your time, thought and sometimes just lending an ear.

These are really short snippets of what each meridian might mean to you and if you are interested there is some great information out there to research.

Which ones are testing weak when you hold your cash against them, or say your statement? Keep a note. Those that are weak will work against you getting your want.

Therefore the logical next step is to correct the weaknesses, strengthen the meridian/s in question so that they begin to support rather than sabotage you in realising your 'wants'.

CORRECTING ANY DISCREPANCIES

One simple way to strengthen a meridian is to trace it with the palm of your hand and a brief description is given below. Or, visit my site www.midlifegoddess.ning.com where there is a video demonstrating meridian tracing.

Central	Place both hands on your pubic bone and bring them straight up the front of your body to your bottom lip. In tracing you can either touch the clothing, or work an inch or so off the body. Both work. The important thing is to relax, focus and tune into the energy.
Governing	Place one hand at your tailbone and trace straight up your spine as high as you can; reach over your shoulder and try to touch the hand reaching up; if your hands cannot meet, simply connect them with your mind, then, with the hand that reached over your shoulder, trace the energy the rest of the way up your spine, over your head, over your nose and end on your top lip.

Spleen	Start at the inside [medial – ie the side of the toe next to the 'air'] corners of each big toe and go straight up the inside of your legs, flaring out at the hips, up the side of the rib cage and down to the bottom of the rib cage.
Heart	Place your open hand underneath the opposite armpit in alignment with your little finger and trace straight down inside the arm and off the little finger – both sides.
Small Intestine	Turn your hand over and, starting at the little finger, go straight up the outside of the arm to your shoulder, drop back on your scapula, go over to the cheekbone, and back to the opening of your ear – do both sides.

Bladder	Place both hands between your eyebrows; go up over the crown and down the back of your head and neck; remove your hands from the neck, reach them back underneath and as high as you can stretch onto your spine; trace your hands down either side of your spine to below your waist, jog in and up towards the waist and then in and around your gluteus maximus [butt]. Leave the meridian there and come up onto your shoulders, go straight down to the back of your knees, in at the knees, down to the floor and off your little toes.
Kidney	Place your fingers under the ball of each foot, middle finger in line with the space between your first and second toes. Draw your fingers up to the inside of each foot, circle behind the inside of each ankle bone. Go straight up the front of the body to K27, the points beneath the clavicle at the top of the sternum; vigorously press and rub these points.

Circulation sex	Place the fingers of one hand at the outside of the opposite nipple. Come up over the shoulder, go down the inside of the arm and off the middle finger, do both sides. When we were training we called this one 'nip to tip'.
Triple Warmer	Turn your hand over and starting at the ring finger, trace straight up the arm to beneath your ear, follow your ear around and behind, ending at your temple. Do both sides.
Gallbladder	Place the fingers of both hands on the outside of your eyes. Drop to the opening of your ears, take your fingers straight up about two inches. Circle forward with your fingers and drop back behind the ears. Go forward again over to your forehead then back over the crown of the head and around the shoulders. Leave the shoulders, bring your hands to the sides of your rib cage, go forward on the rib cage, back on the waist, forward on the hips and straight down the sides of the legs and off the fourth toes.

Liver	Place your fingers on the outsides [lateral side next to second toe] of your big toes and trace straight up inside the legs, flaring out at your hips, up the sides of your rib cage and back to underneath your ribs, in line with your nipples.
Lung	Place one hand over the opposite lung and move it up over your shoulder, straight down your arm, and off your thumb – do both sides.
Large Intestine	Place the open fingers of one hand at the end of the index finger of the opposite hand. Trace straight up the finger, the arm to your shoulder, cross the neck to beneath your nose and go out to the flair of your nose – do on both sides.
Stomach	Place both hands underneath your eyes. Drop down to your jawbone. Circle up the outside of your face to your forehead. Come down through your eyes to the collarbone. Go out at your collarbone, over your breasts, in at your waist, out at the hops, straight down the legs and off the second toes.

CREATIVE CORRECTIONS

This section just gives you the titles of the corrections, for reference only. Go to the section at the end of the book for full descriptions.

You can also correct each meridian by slowly and deliberately tracing the pathway and saying the affirmation below.

Tracing is following the pathway with an open palm [of your hand] – think of it like a little electromagnetic pad and once you align it with the meridian, the energy connects to it and moves with it.

So stand, take a few deep breaths, root yourself into the earth, rub your hands together and shake them off and then place the palms on the beginning of the meridian; focus and feel a connection and then slowly follow the pathway.

You are not inserting needles into acupoints so therefore you don't have to be pinpoint accurate, just follow the instructions above [or the You Tube Clip on my site] and focus and hold your intention – a HUGE percentage of energy work is intention.

You only need to correct the meridians that tested
weak,
not all of them.

As you do the corrections; smile, breathe and say

**"I love money and money loves me,
it comes into my life with total ease,
in the most divine way and all is well"**

Central	Empty out, Zip and sew up
Governing	Classic Hook up
Stomach	3 Mile point with side bend
Spleen	Monkey thumping
Heart	Massage Heart 8 – The genie in your hand 9 hearts with affirmations
Small Intestine	Massage the source point
Bladder	Rub vigorously Bladder 1-3 several times
Kidney	K27
Circ Sex	Inner gate master point
Triple Warmer	Teddy Boy Sweep
Gallbladder	Massage GB20 – the Wind Pool
Liver	Rub Neurolymphatic reflex points ~~then rake out to Lung 1 and 2 and massage firmly~~
Lung	Rub Neurolymphatic reflex points on the sternum then rake out to Lung 1 and 2 and massage firmly
Large Intestine	Massage firmly the outside of each thigh, where the seams of your trousers lie.

Retest each meridian against the money
and it should test strong.

NOW RETEST YOUR ORIGINAL 'WANT'
STATEMENT
– is it strong now?

At this point I would say that 85%

of you need go no further. You have cleared the main
stumbling block [money] that was stopping you
achieving your 'want' – be happy, confident, optimistic,
do your homework [see below] and enjoy achieving
your desires in life.

WEAVING TOGETHER YOUR DAILY WEALTH WORKOUT

If it is now strong, then there was an underlying issue about money that was getting in the way. You have removed it but you need to keep it out of the way, don't allow it to sneak back in and sabotage your 'want' or your bank balance.

You need to do your daily wealth workout – twice a day for three or four weeks. Your Daily Wealth Workout will be the exercises you used to balance the meridians against the money [or statement] + the following affirmation and tapping.

Draw on your discipline to do this. Often we don't do things when we KNOW they will help us, that is because we are out of balance in some way. However, you will be gaining a balance so it should be easier to find the focus you need to do them, do them consistently and do them with a smile.

Say the following statement every morning and evening after you clean your teeth – look at yourself in the mirror, smile and say it 6 times while tapping the apex of your cheeks.

'I now love and attract money to me and money loves me and is attracted to me in the most divine way. I'm getting rich!

– all is well.'

Keep doing this for 3-4 weeks to really embed this new energetic thought field around the issue of money in your life. It is said to take 21 days to change a habit of any kind; add a few more to be on the safe side.

To ensure that you don't slip back into the issue of money sabotaging you. Get tested or self test, every week to ensure you remain strong on the statement.

Money is a good, positive thing [should test strong]
Money is a bad, negative thing [should test weak]

Timing: well, the devil is in the timing as they say. Your 'want' could materialise very quickly or it may take its time. Objectively evaluate regularly: is your want coming into your orbit?

So in summary:

You test to make sure you have no major subconscious hang up about money.

You test to see how each of your meridians reacts to the idea of having money – any weakness will give you valuable insight into why money is not flowing into your life.

You correct any issues found.

You could stop there, but to truly cover your options let's see if you feel you DESERVE to have money and that your subconscious believes it is SAFE to have it... proceed to Part 2.

PART TWO

YOU'RE DEFINITELY WORTH IT AND IT'S SAFE

Let's cover all options.
Energy test these two statements:

1 – I deserve to have lots of money
2 – It's safe for me to have lots of money

Are you weak on either of these?
Then you need to work with the techniques in this section

You can also adapt these techniques to work directly on your 'want', once you are strong on money.

You are definitely worth it!

Ok, so what if you still test weak on money? What if you are testing strong on money but it doesn't hold for long?
Then it is worthwhile exploring this section about feeling that you 'deserve' money and that having money is safe, it represents no danger whatsoever.

Once you test strong on money then retest your 'want'.
The money issue is your real cornerstone so you have to ensure that is firm, strong and supportive before you even address your 'want'.

Our next port of call is to see if you [and your mini-me[9]] feel, with every fibre of your body, that you actually DESERVE to have money.

Simply say the statement:

'I now deserve to have lots of money'

If this statement tests strong there is not an issue about you being worthy or deserving.

---

9 Mini-me is the name I give to that part of you that is beyond your consciousness.

However, if this statement tests weak then there is an issue that needs to be addressed. You need to reconstruct your self esteem

Say the following statement every morning and evening after you clean your teeth – look at yourself in the mirror, smile and say it 6 times while tapping the apex of your cheeks.

'I deserve and am 100% worthy of having money it now comes to me easily. I'm enjoying this – all is well.'

Keep doing this for 3-4 weeks to embed this new energetic thought field around the issue of being deserving. You will feel a difference way before then, but it is a safeguard.

To ensure that you don't slip back into feeling undeserving, get tested or self test, every week to ensure you remain strong on the statement.

The whole issue of self worth/self esteem can be one doozie of a stumbling block that we can trip over and fall flat on our little faces.

Does your sub conscious [your mini-me] really believe you deserve to have plenty of money?

Start valuing yourself or be undervalued by others.

There is not a shred of shame in having plenty of money or getting what you want, contrary to our conditioning; there is no virtue in self denial or poverty.

TECHNIQUES TO HELP YOU FEEL SAFE

It could be that part of you does not feel 'safe' around the issue. An area of your mind, *beyond your conscious control*, the area I call Mini-Me for some misguided reason does not want you to succeed. Mini-Me is sabotaging you every step of the way, in fact it will stop you even starting.

This area of your subconscious should be your inner voice of wisdom. The sage within that keeps you alive and healthy.

However, through trauma or stressful experiences, this inner wise woman can become the voice of fear, a little gremlin, determined to undermine your efforts because for some misguided reason it believes those efforts threaten your very survival. If it perceives that you are in danger, it will become distressed and activate any response to change your course of action.

Mini-Me has a profound power over us and an astonishing array of tactics to sabotage our efforts: metabolism can be slowed to a state of walking hibernation; our memories fail us; we become cynical around the subject we wish to change.

Common sense tells us that having plenty of money or achieving your 'want' does not threaten your life or anyone else's, but Mini-Me thinks it might, it's thought process has ceased to be logical and has entered the realms of complex fantasy. In the Kingdom of Mini-me; having plenty of money represents a serious threat to your health, in fact your very survival !!! it is spelling 'red alert' and exclamation marks.

I would stress again, that this is totally outside your conscious control.

How can you persuade Mini-Me to start supporting you in achieving money and your 'want'? Reprogramming is the answer. We need to rewire the connections and associations. To that end I want to share with you a simple generic technique that over many years, with many clients I have found to have a neurological effect that is effective in persuading Mini-Me that it is safe to change particular habits.

Of course you may not have a sabotaging Mini-Me but I still recommend that you work with this technique; it will do no harm and strengthen an already balanced Mini-Me.

Make your statement. For example: 'It is now safe for me to have plenty of money' and test [as described earlier, either with a friend or self testing].

If it tests strong

you do not have a general problem with Mini-Me around the issue of having plenty of money but

If it tests weak

Mini-Me is behaving like a gremlin not a sage. To double check just test again saying: *'It is now not safe for me to have plenty of money'* – if this tests strong it confirms you have a gremlin in the works, a real life, gold plated psychological reversal. Getting money into your life and achieving your want is going to be like pushing water uphill. You definitely need to reprogramme.

Working on the premise that Mini-Me needs to *feel safe* around the issue of having plenty of money [or your want] you directly reassure Mini-Me with affirmations[10] made with smiles and specific tapping points.

This is how you do it...

Say *'it is now safe for me to have plenty of money – all is well'* 6 times, looking at yourself in the mirror, smiling widely, camping it up a bit and tapping the points on the apex of your cheeks.

---

10 The influence of the mind on the body's health is well-established. In a thirty-five year longitudinal study, people with a pessimistic explanatory style were at greater risk for physical illness than individuals with an optimistic explanatory style. The power of thought on biological processes is decisive and direct. Focused intention can literally wind or unwind the tightness of DNA strands, leading to speculation that DNA acts as an "antenna" attuned to fields and thought processes that ultimately influence the expression of specific genes.

 The statement works as an affirmation, reprogramming behaviour. The wide smile encourages the release of endorphins [the body's 'happy hormones'] into the system, which Mini-Me then associates with the affirmation. At the same time, tapping the cheek points [Stomach 3 shown in above photo] reduces anxiety around the affirmation, making it easier to be accepted by Mini-Me.

In the first three to four weeks, the more you do this, the more effective it will be and the quicker you will achieve results.

Do it a minimum of twice a day to persuade Mini-Me that it is a good idea to have loads of money or to achieve your 'want'. Sometimes the groove of self sabotage can run deep, it may take time to climb out of that groove, but be assured ... you can and you will!

Don't be timid, face Mini-Me openly and with total belief in your success.

You can say it by itself, in your head [i.e. without the smiling and tapping] as many times a day as you wish, the more the better. Try it next time you are stuck in a queue at the bank, supermarket or traffic lights.

Shhhhh... a secret tap

To keep yourself on track, if you find yourself slipping, here is a great emotional first aid technique using a Triple Warmer[11] acupressure point.

I call it the **SECRET TAP** as it can be done discreetly anywhere, anytime you feel stressed about your issue.

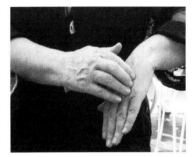

- take a deep breath and smile
- say a positive statement such as: *'all is well, it's happening, timing is divine and money is coming to me'*
- at the same time tap the top of your left hand at the base of the little finger and ring finger knuckles
- keep tapping for about 15econds to give yourself a quick fix

Australian Bush Flower[12] remedy FIVE CORNERS, is said to release negative beliefs, increase self esteem and confidence, empower and strengthen affirmations. It can really help stop you self sabotaging. Most good health food stores will be able to obtain this for you. If not, try the Nutricentre Mail order section.[13]

---

11 The Triple Warmer meridian, that runs from the 'ring finger' up the arm, neck, behind, up and over the ear, ending at the temples, is associated with stress, by tapping it you are reducing the stress response around the issue.

12 Devised in Australia by Ian White, these are powerful flower essences – I love them, check out Black Eyed Susan, one of the best for stress. www.ausflowers.com

13 Sometimes it is convenient to order online: www.NutriCentre.com

TEDDY BOY SWEEP – an alternative to tapping

This is an alternative technique to the cheek tapping, for reducing the stress response around your 'want'.

Rather than tapping your cheeks you will be aligning the energy of your hands with the end of the Triple Warmer meridian, on each temple. Once aligned you trace backwards along part of the pathway. Working in this direction, calms and sedates the energy around the issue.

Place the palms of each hand against each temple.

Take a deep breath in and as you breathe out trace the hands up the front of the ear, over the top and down behind the ear. Down the neck to the point where a necklace would naturally fall, pull off firmly along that necklace line and end by shaking off both hands.

Do this a couple of times and you will instantly feel calmer. In fact as a species, many of us, irrelevant of culture, automatically do the beginning part of the

 Teddy Boy Sweep when we feel overwhelmed or stressed in any way.

NOW RETEST your statement [be in about your money or your want]

it should be strong.

Phew! You've addressed the money issue, self esteem and safety; Mini-me is finally on your side and will help rather than hinder you.

You are all set – fast-track to your dreams.

The only thing left to do is ...

SET YOURSELF HOMEWORK

YOUR DAILY WEALTH WORKOUT

Teddy boy sweep and the statement [+ smile] twice a day for at least ten days. Testing yourself all the time to ensure the reprogramming is working. It can take up to 3-4 weeks for the statement to hold firmly all the time; thus indicating a successful reprogramming.

Trace Regulator Flow at the end of your homework [see explanation later in the book or on You Tube]

**Still weak when you test for
money or your 'want' ?**

And yes, it occasionally is.

Then we may need to dig even deeper,

there could be a more specific

psychological reversal around

money and/or your want?

Take a look at the next section

PART THREE

STOP THE FEAR

THAT'S STOPPING YOU

This is more in-depth work and addresses chronic emotional problems emerging from some deep rooted 'fear' around either having money or achieving your 'want'.

You will need this section if:

1 – you can't get a strong test on money after any of the preceding techniques, or

2 – your money issue is now strong but your 'want' still tests weak.

DO YOU REALLY WANT IT ?

Is there a psychological reversal going on?

What's the fear that feeds it?

I have found that all psychological reversals are fed by our fears. Often by *layers* of complex fears. It can seem sometimes that not even years of therapy will subdue these fears.

However, using this simple energy testing technique, you can identify the PRIORITY FEAR that is core to the problem. This fear will be feeding your gremlin of self sabotage and prevent money coming into your life easily and/or you achieving your 'want'.

Study the fears on the following 'PRIORITY FEAR LIST' and identify the ones that you suspect may be associated with your possible issue around your want – *I'll use 'want' in this section but it can equally apply to the money issue.*

Verbally confirm that you are testing your subconscious to discover the PRIORITY FEAR related to the psychological reversal around your 'want'. It is important that you are clear on this fact as there may be layers of fears, you can't deal with all of them at once, so you are seeking the most important one, the priority at this moment.

So you would be setting the energetic field by saying:

***"I now want to identify the key priority fear
around the issue of changing my job
– I seek the truth"***

*[Remember, there can only be ONE priority! You seek
the truth and what you do with that truth is 100% up
to you: YOU are in control all the time]*

You might like to make your own list of fears, but I offer
you mine as a start point. Test what instinctively you
feel may be the problem first. You may want to change
the vocabulary – do so as just a subtle change can make
a big difference to the meaning for your Mini-me.

Now there are an awful lot of fears to test so I have a
cunning technique to make it easier for you.

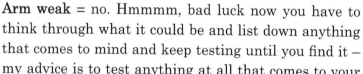

First put your hand on the **entire list** and ask the question:

Is the priority fear around my issue of blah blah blah
on this list?

Arm strong = yes – in which case proceed to ❶

Arm weak = no. Hmmmm, bad luck now you have to
think through what it could be and list down anything
that comes to mind and keep testing until you find it –
my advice is to test anything at all that comes to your
mind, however 'silly' you might judge it to be. Once you
have it, proceed to reprogramming and make sure you
add that fear onto the list, in this way it becomes truly
comprehensive.

❶ test each 'block' [shaded below to demonstrate] and say:

Is the priority fear around my issue of blah blah blah in this block.

Arm strong = yes proceed to ❷

Arm weak = no proceed to next block until you find the block where your arm goes strong and then proceed to ❷

❷ Once you have located your block, find your **row** by testing each one.

Is the priority fear around my issue of blah blah blah in this row?

If arm is strong = fear in that row – go to ❸

If arm is weak – repeat on next row until you find the one that contains your priority fear and the go to ❸

❸ Now at this point, things change slightly, you stop asking a question and instead just say the fear statement and the test will measure what it does to your energy. How will your energy react when you bring that fear to mind and voice it?

So – say out loud: '*FEAR OF BEING LOVED*' [or whatever your priority fear is] and energy test.

It should test WEAK – confirming you have found your priority fear and remember, there can only be one.

I know this sounds complicated the first time you read it, but just follow the instructions and they will guide you through to your very important discovery. When you have done it once, you will realise how easy and logical it is.

Ideally you will have a friend to test you, but if you have nobody around and don't want to wait – you can use the self testing technique in the first section.[14]

EXAMPLES OF PRIORITY FEARS TO BE TESTED

Abandon- ment	Socially acceptable	Taking risks	Boredom
Being dependent	Change	Being a victim	Being hurt emotionally
Helpless- ness	Death	Violence	Being hurt physically
Being vulnerable	Communica- tion	Addiction	Being hurt mentally

14 If you are interesting in energy testing and would like more information on how to get really good at it – contact Madison for a comprehensive pdf eBooklet with everything you need to know!

Being ignored	Standing out from the crowd	attention	Emotionally abused
Being rejected	Being adequate	Pain	Verbally abused
Trusting	Misunderstood	Ageing	Touch
Loving	Accepted for yourself	Being ugly	Sex
Being loved	Lonely	Illness	Being attractive
Being in love	Dependency upon you	Confusion	Being deserving
Being unloved	Being dependent	Unworthy	Anonymity
Grief	Judgement	Not being understood	Belonging
Insanity	Defining boundaries	Not being accepted	Self-worth
Taking personal power	Being limited by self	In danger	Emotional security
Taking control	Being limited by others	Restrained	Not fulfilling your destiny
Losing control	Being wanted	Lack of freedom	Walking your truth
Success	Forgiveness	Starving	Talking your truth
Being centre of attention	Betrayed	Hunger	Being an individual
Commitment	Found guilty	Responsibilities	Taking risks

Receiving	Laughed at	Moving forward	Failure
Being happy	Taking opportunities	Growth	Emotional insecurity
Being unhappy	Missing opportunities	Achieving ambitions	Loss of independence

If you are a therapist and would like to work with this technique you may feel it worthwhile to invest the time and effort into making up little laminated cards with a fear on each and use them to discover the priority fear issue. Simply place your hand on the deck and ask if the priority fear is in it. Should test strong. Then cut the deck in two test each to see where the priority fear lies, cut again and do the same. Keep doing this until you get down to half a dozen then test each one.

How to reprogramme
Set the fear free, you no longer need it in your life

You have identified that there is a psychological reversal present around your 'want' and the priority fear it is feeding on.

You now need to reassure your subconscious that it is safe to let go of that fear, that the fear is now inappropriate. You will persuade it to *support* you in creating the reality of your choice rather than work against you. To help you achieve your 'want' as quickly as possible.

This technique is best done in silence, with both of you focusing fully on the fear. An easy way to keep this focus, is to both keep repeating the fear out loud – 'fear of being loved, fear of being loved, fear of being loved' keep your voice and face expressionless, you are simply holding the energy of the priority fear.

As you have seen, simply 'saying' the fear puts your energy in a weakened state. Therefore, this technique addresses the energy in its weakened, imbalanced form and encourages it NOT re react to the fear by going out of balance, it pulls it back into harmony, whilst facing the fear (or thought of the fear). You are effectively 'reprogramming' the energy body's reaction to this issue, restoring the default 'factory setting'.

Sit or lie quietly, repeating the fear, whilst your partner gently holds the NEUROVASCULAR[15] points on your forehead. Stay in this position, until he/she can feel a synchronised pulse under their fingers. This can take 1 minute or 20. *If you are alone, you can do this on yourself.*

Once your partner/ you feels the pulse, he/she/you will tap the Stomach points[16] on your cheek for 20 seconds.

---

15 These are simply points located on the head that can calm and balance the organ or system associated with them. The ones we are using are specifically for stress.

16 Tapping these Stomach points helps alleviate anxiety around the issue., a slightly different way of dealing with the stress.

End by holding the Triple Warmer sedation points [shown on the next page] until you feel a steady pulse. If you are not sure of how to hold these points visit You Tube, tap in Madison King Triple Warmer and up I'll pop demonstrating it for you.

There are myriad simple techniques to sedate Triple Warmer. This one does take a little more effort, but is well worth it as it is a potent stress reliever and if you think about it, nearly everything thing that can go wrong with us is stress related, so these little points can help almost anything – you never have to feel helpless again – just hold the points to achieve your want or to help heal your body!

Do not get too hung up on exactly where the points are – that in itself can sometimes cause anxiety. You are not inserting needles, so with a broad hand and lots of attention, intention and focus you will cover the area you need to cover.

SIT COMFORTABLY AND HOLD THE FIRST SET OF POINTS ON THE LEFT HAND SIDE OF THE BODY

BREATHE DEEPLY. KEEP HOLDING UNTIL YOU BEGIN TO FEEL A GENTLE YET FIRM PULSE IN EACH POINT

HOLD THE SECOND SET OF POINTS ON THE LEFT SIDE OF THE BODY

So you have held two sets of points on the left hand side of the body and then two sets on the right hand side. If you feel drawn to holding one set on the left, then one set on the right then holding the second set on the left and then on the right, that will work too – it is really a case of what you feel drawn to do.

If you are under specific stress, you may need to hold these points for more than a few seconds, perhaps two or three minutes each until you feel a light pulse in the points, this is the signal that the energy is changing. Be guided by your instinct.

Holding pressure is light. Use 2-3 fingers to hold the area of each point. Or if you prefer, use the SIMPLE WAY with the whole hand.

Points to hold are :–

1st pair – Triple Warmer 10 and Stomach 36

2nd pair – Triple Warmer 2 and Bladder 66

TRIPLE WARMER 10
When the elbow is flexed, about one thumb width above the bend on the outside.

SIMPLE WAY: wrap your hand around your elbow. Think of standing like a genie

STOMACH 36
About 3 fingers below the kneecap
And 1 finger to the outside – you'll feel a little indentation.

SIMPLE WAY: wrap hand around top of lower leg

TRIPLE WARMER 2
In the web between 4th and 5th fingers

SIMPLE WAY: place palm over 4th and 5th knuckles, fingertips curling over the edge of the hand and touching palm.

BLADDER 66
In the indentation on the side of the foot just below the edge of the little toe.

SIMPLE WAY: hold the edge of your foot so that the palm is over the little toe
[again, if you are a visual person – take a look on You Tube[17] to 'see' the holding points].
Retest the fear and you should be strong.

---

17 Also available in the video section on my site
www.midlifegoddess.ning.com

Retest your statement (*e.g. want to work less and earn more money*) and you should be strong. If not, simply repeat the above process, it needs more time to integrate the change.

Maybe trace Regulator Flow [in next section and a video on my site too if you prefer to watch rather than read. This will help you regulate and adjust to the changes]

RETEST YOU WILL BE STRONG!

All that remains for you to do is your homework!

This will be your affirmation with either the forehead holding points, *or* tapping the cheeks *or* Teddy Boy Sweep. Always smiling and camping it up slightly as you say them.

End with tracing Regulator flow [see instructions later in the book or tap in Madison Regulator Flow on You Tube and watch me do it].

Do this for a couple of weeks – keep testing to make sure your original want statement is still testing strong.

If at any time it tests weak again it may be that you have fixed that particular fear and another little gremlin causing a psychological reversal is raising its head. In which case repeat the procedure. Occasionally this happens.

Always test your affirmations to be 100% sure they are having the desired effect. Sometimes it can be just a simple change of words that make it effective.

Don't fall over another stumbling block that is called 'over 'analysis and procrastination'. Find it, fix it, do your homework and move on to your want. [18] You are learning how to love it, learn from it and let it go. You have achieved this, nobody else, you have healed and empowered yourself and now have tools that you can use for the rest of your life. Doesn't that feel good?

---

18 Wish I could claim this one as 100% my own but it originates from Elizabeth Lovius 'agent of change' : *When S*** happens, Love it, Lead it, Leave it* – enjoy her site and blog on: **www.elizabethlovius. com**

PART FOUR

Putting together your

Daily Wealth Workout

Key techniques and some optional fun extras.

Select the ones that are indicated for you [i.e. that strengthen any meridian weakness] or that simply read well to you and that you feel drawn to. The secret of your Wealth Workout is to make it something that you enjoy, if you enjoy it, you'll do it and that is the key to the success of your wealth plan.

A little light relief now with some
PROSPERITY TIPS

Words of wisdom that I have collected over the years.
They are fun and I thought you might enjoy them –
read through and try those that make you smile.

1. Define with absolute clarity what you want and need.

2. Clear out clutter from your home, office, car and mind.

3. Take a brisk walk every day for 20 minutes – it will keep you positive – say your affirmations or enjoy day dreaming and visualising achieving your 'wants'. Thinking is one thing, 'imagining' is another – it expands the energy around your 'want', this in turn attracts things to it to turn it from an imagining into a reality.

4. Keep revisiting your strategy for 'want' manifestation – give it energy – do something every day to bring you one step closer.

5. Positive self-talk in fact, positive talk in all ways.

6. Keep your loo seat and lid firmly down [men take note], so that your good fortune is not flushed away.

7. Water is a symbol of wealth in some Oriental countries – make sure all your plumbing is sound and there are no leaks [otherwise money could leak out of your life unnecessarily].

8. The Water in your body – bladder represents the home of hope, positivity and optimism – take care of your internal waterworks.

9. Treat yourself to the best red purse you can afford – a touch of luxury sends a positive message to the Universe and red is a colour that is associated with wealth. Alternatively there is a school of thought that believes a purse should be green as this signifies growth. What feels right for you – go with your instinct.

10. Wrap up in red paper the highest denomination note you have. Keep it in your purse to attract money.

11. Put a citrine or Tiger's Eye crystal in your purse to do the same.

12. Three Chinese coins tied with a red ribbon attract money.

13. Three coins, all of the same type help you avoid wasting money unnecessarily. I have three replica Roman coins in my wallet.

14. I don't know if this is legal but I have done it for years: when you open up your spanking new cheque book write the first cheque out to yourself for ten million pounds and sign it 'The Univeral Banker' –

you can pin that cheque on your fridge or info board – somewhere where you will see it.

15. Always carry cash in your purse and wallet, never leave them empty.

16. Always accept gifts with grace, even if it is just a friend paying for a cup of coffee. If you refuse, the Universal Banker thinks you don't want help anymore!

17. I know this is hard for some of us but try and do something you love. You will do it well and provide something that other people will enjoy be it a product or service; if you enjoy it, it is more likely to be a success and if you love it, it adds an energetic value to it.

18. Keep brooms, mop or the vacuum cleaner out of sight. This prevents your fortune being 'brushed away'.

19. Find your abundance/prosperity/wealth corner in your house and in each room and put some money in it, or a plant [represents growth], or a picture/collage of what you want, or a fish [represents water which in turn represent wealth].

20. Give money away – it starts the flow.

21. Don't try and double guess your Universal Piggy Bank. Your job is to 'ask', UPB's job is to find a way to manifest your want and the ways can be quite inventive sometimes!

22. Hang out with positive, creative, prosperous, successful friends. Of course, friends have problem times too and you need to be supportive, but overall, friends should uplift your energy.

WEALTH		
↑	Entrance of house or individual room	↑

23. Amethyst enhances your 'wealth corner'.

24. Write down your affirmation and put it in your wealth corner.

25. Get a Chinese lucky frog with a coin in its mouth and place it in your wealth corner.

26. KUA numbers for prosperity. I was teaching in Cardiff one weekend; the wonderful thing about workshops is that we all learn from each other and one of the students[19] was a Feng Shui expert and he shared with us the basic calculation to find your personal Kua number which in turn tells you what directions bring in good positive energy into your life and those that don't. This has an impact on the directions you work, walk, sit and sleep. Could changing the direction of your desk bring in more money and success? Try it and see.

The formula is different for men and women – Google it for full instructions but basically for a woman:

19 Thank you 'L' – you know who you are and know I always love your morsels of knowledge x

- Take the year of your birth and add together the last 2 digits.
- If the result is 10 or more, add the 2 digits to reduce them to a single number, then add 5.
- If the result is 10 or more, add the two digits to reduce them to a single number
- This number is your personal KUA number.

For example: If you were born in 1960
6+0 = 6
6+5 = 11
1+1 = 2 [your Kua number]

Now check out the table below to check out your best directions.

If you don't have a compass handy, go on Google Maps and tap in your house, it will show a compass/direction indicator, so you can work out the basic directions.

Can you move your bed so the crown of your head is facing a good direction? If it is impossible don't worry – nothing awful is going to happen. Possibly better that your feet don't face the door, which the Chinese believe is not good for you, but it is all a matter of keeping it in perspective ... although I am a stickler for keeping my clocks going on time and putting down the loo seat so my luck does not get flushed away!

After the workshop I went straight home and changed the position of my desk – it does look slightly strange and I notice people looking at it wondering why on earth it is where it is ... but I cannot deny that since I changed it, life has become very busy and abundant!

YOUR BEST DIRECTION FOR MONEY AND SUCCESS WILL BE:

1	**South east**
2	**Northeast**
3	**South**
4	**North**
5 female	**Southwest**
5 male	**Northeast**
6	**West**
7	**Northwest**
8	**Southwest**
9	**East**

Hope you enjoyed that brief interlude, now back to work!

RECOGNISING THE POWER OF THOUGHT

Try this simple exercise with a friend, which may shock you as it demonstrates the immense power of thought and the spoken word.

Have your friend stand in front of you and think [or say] something negative e.g. *I really don't like that colour blouse on you, I don't like that lipstick, You look dreadful today* – whatever it is, make it a real negative!

[the temptation is to smile, don't – smiling strengthens the energies, you don't want that to happen, you want to see exactly how her energy reacts].

Put your arm out into the testing position and have your friend energy test you immediately after making the statement.

You will test weak – just the negative thought/words have thrown your energies out ... such is the power of thought (and the spoken word).

Of course, the reverse is true – say something wonderful to somebody and you immediately boost their energies – do it to yourself in the mirror – smile and feel the difference it makes.

You can use this to your advantage with **affirmations**.

Some suggestions to empower your affirmations:-

- Keep them *short*

- Vital that they are *positive*

- Put them in the *present* tense

- Use your *own wording*, it will more accurately reflect what you feel and therefore have more power (however, some samples are set out below to inspire you).

- Say the affirmation in your *mother tongue.* This is a highly individual aspect of affirmations – play safe and test the affirmation in English first and then in your Mother Tongue – see which one strengthens you. If they both do then simply choose the one you like working in.

- Allow yourself some *quiet time*, in a space where you will not be interrupted. Early morning, before the day starts getting crazy, in the bath, before falling asleep, or a favourite with me is to do them when I am walking, in the rhythm of my steps. Or sitting by the ocean watching the waves – Water is new beginnings and that is what you want!

- Take the time you feel you need. It could be one minute, it could be an hour.

- Take some deep *calming breaths* and try to quiet the chattering of you mind. You might like to light a candle, or an incense stick. *Making a ritual* in this way, focuses the mind and therefore increases the power of the affirmation.

- Decide upon your affirmation and *write it down*. Committing it to paper can make it more effective. It should be the only thing written on that paper.

- Call your '*Inner self*' before you make your affirmation. Just say your name slowly, concentrating on it, three times.

- Make your affirmation as many times in the day as possible. You can even do it when you are stuck in a traffic jam. They don't always have to be OM and bliss!) Basically, the more you repeat the affirmation, the more likely your mind will take it on board and changes will begin to occur.

- Use affirmations at any time during the course of the day.

- *SMILE* as you say them, this stimulates endorphins and lifts your mood.

- Consider using the Australian Bush Flower remedy *FIVE CORNERS,* which is said to empower and strengthen affirmations.

- Trace *Regulator* immediately before and after your affirmation session, to encourage integration. [instructions at the end and also on You Tube]

- Don't spend 5 minutes making a positive affirmation and then 23 hours and 55 minutes thinking negative thoughts!

- Don't be insipid or wish washy. No maybes, ifs, buts or perhaps. Be certain, firm and doubtless.

- Don't be a moaning Minnie, you are now dealing in solutions not problems or blocks.

- Shoot the arrow, forget it and trust it. Literally, let go and let your Universal Piggy Bank take care of you.

YOU WILL GET WHAT YOU EXPECT, SO DO NOT EXPECT FAILURE; EXPECT TOTAL SUCCESS, YOU WILL GET YOUR WANT ... DON'T DOUBT IT !

As you trust there will be air for your next breath, trust your want will manifest itself.

TURBO TAPPING   – *totally optional*

Affirmations can be further strengthened by Temple Turbo Tapping.

A technique for anchoring positive goals and changes into the 'present'. It helps break old habits and encourage new behaviour patterns.

Tapping the temple area, temporarily switches off incoming sensory filtering and makes you more receptive to the repetition of the affirmation, to the auto-suggestion.

It brings the brain's attention to what you are saying.

It sedates Triple Warmer (you are tapping along part of the meridian), which in turn puts you in a more relaxed and receptive mode.

There are two hemispheres to the brain, which react in different ways, so two statements (affirmations) are used.

RIGHT   **LEFT**

More positive, non-linear and open to ideas. Responds more effectively to statements using a positive wording.	More critical and sceptical. Accepts a statement in the 'negative' wording more easily.

Determine two statements, conveying the same meaning. One should be positive, the other should have a positive meaning but employ 'negative' wording.

Put your palms on your temples and smooth them up, over and behind your ears, down the back of your neck and off your shoulders. At the same time, breathing deeply. [recognise the Teddy Boy Sweep that is calming down Triple Warmer and making you more receptive to the suggestions].

Quiet your mind, you need to pay attention to what you are doing. The more focus you bring, the more effective the technique.

 **RIGHT POSITIVE**

 **LEFT NEGATIVE**

Using your RIGHT HAND, starting at the right temple, going up, over and down behind the ear; FIRMLY TAP, while stating the POSITIVE statement in rhythm with your tapping. Say the words in rhythm with your tapping. Smile. Repeat 5/6 TIMES	Take your LEFT HAND, starting at the LEFT TEMPLE, going up, over and behind the ear, FIRMLY TAP your head whilst stating the NEGATIVELY worded statement. Say the words in rhythm with your tapping. Smile. Repeat 5/6 TIMES
Money comes easily into my life with no stress at all. I love the way money comes to me so effortlessly now. I finally trust that I have enough money now and always. I now have a deep knowing that the Universe supports me totally. I now embrace the belief that the Universe will provide all I need and want. I now love and trust my Universal Piggy Bank! It is good to take time out for me.	I no longer feel I have to work so hard. I don't doubt that I have and will always have more than enough money. I'm not worried and no longer fear that I won't be able to support myself. I don't fear poverty as I am rich. I no longer think money is a bad thing I'm not a bad person if I take some time out for myself. I no longer doubt the Universe.

End by repeating the first step. Teddy Boy Sweep and tracing Regulator Flow while saying: *"All is well, I am safe, protected and cared for"*. Or whatever statement conveys this meaning for you.

This should take a couple of minutes. Repeat several times a day, every day. After a while, it will begin to 'reprogramme' your brain. It only works if you do it with attention, intention and consistently over a period of weeks. On average, you should begin to feel its effect after about 3 weeks, if not before, as I said before, it takes 21 days to change a habit.

PICTURE IT

Imagine yourself sitting in an armchair, with a huge screen in front of you.

The screen turns on and you are on the centre of it. You are smiling and laughing as money [or whatever it is you want] comes pouring into the screen with you.

You are getting what you wanted. What does it look like in glorious Technicolor? How does it feel? How does it smell? Can you touch it? Bring all your senses to this visualisation.

 Smile, close your eyes and imagine a huge tick over the image. Stamp a giant 'YES!' over that.

Feel the joy and tap your 3rd eye gently with your fingertips for 5 seconds.

Take a deep breath – open your eyes, smile and know that what you want is on its way.

END ANY OF THE TECHNIQUES BY TAKING 15/20 SECONDS TO TRACE THE REGULATOR FLOW

The Regulator flow is part of the ancient Strangeflows system of energies, also known as: radiant circuits; curious conduits; collector meridians; extraordinary vessels; inner wells of joy; wondrous flows and psychic channels.

Strangeflows were first mentioned in Chinese texts 4,000 years ago. Taoist yoga continues the tradition but for some unknown reason, Strangeflows are rarely used in the West and for this reason I am including a brief explanation of these radiant circuits of energy.

Thought to be the 'original' energy flows, Strangeflows are the most powerful, yet subtle flows of the body...

- They are **channels/conduits** of energy that flow through and around the body.
- Unlike meridians which could be thought of as fixed 'motorways' of energy, Strangeflows do not follow fixed routes, and share acupressure points with the meridians they cross.
- They appear to be capable of intelligent choice and can **network** anywhere in the body. They are the original 'trouble-shooters' and will go where they are most needed.

- They respond instantly to thought/visualisation, they are like energetic hyperlinks.
- They monitor, regulate, adjust and tweak the main meridians and associated organs.
- They patrol your energy systems and organs and encourage them to function as a 'true team', working for the **common good** and ready to respond to the challenges life presents.
- Strangeflows mobilise your **INNER MUM** ... Awakening true caring and the spirit of love.
- The energy that is carried on these Strangeflows can be associated with: strength, resilience, joy, vitality, repair, orgasm, support, rapture, exhilaration, hope, gratitude, peace, balance, inspiration, falling in love, spiritual ecstasy.

The Regulator flow is the co-ordinator of the system, it is vital in helping us regulate and adjust to change. You are initiating a change in your core beliefs, so having Regulator flowing at full force is an enormous bonus.

This flow connects with all twelve organ meridians. Think of it like a parent, helping the children [meridians] regulating and supporting each child and maintaining a harmonious communication and cooperation between them all. So bringing it into play after doing your exercises makes them that much more effective. What else does it do?

- It turns on and co-ordinates it all!
- Relevant to any auto-immune problem [when energies are not communicating with each other or adjusting correctly].

- Always related to the Thyroid.
- Influences: hormones, chemistry and circulation.
- Helps adapt/cope with all internal and external changes.
- Establishes harmony with other people and within the environment.
- Helps you adjust to any environmental change.
- Helps you absorb and integrate the benefits of any energy exercise / balance / affirmation and therefore achieve your 'want'.

I am going to describe how you trace the Regulator Flow. I hope you will find my description, while unorthodox, easy to remember. You can also go onto You Tube and click in Madison King Regulator and I'm there demonstrating it.

Your hands are like electromagnetic pads, they have an electromagnetic field extending beyond the skin, and placed over the body, they will align with the energy and move it.

Tracing the front of the body Stand tall, relaxed and take a deep breath.

Place middle fingers between the eyebrows.

Trace a Heart around the edge of the face, ending at the centre of the chin.

Trace down the neck, as if the heart was sitting 'on a stick'.

Cross arms like a 'genie', grasping upper arms, with little fingers level with the elbow crease.

Uncross the arms into a Pharaoh position upwards and over the chest then move them to the side of the breasts – think of Marilyn Munroe!

Trace down the front of the body with a little wiggle - 'Oh I'm so beautiful'. Smile.

Finish by squeezing big and little toes together.

TRACING THE BACK OF THE BODY

Start with the 'Teddy Boy Sweep'. *Palm of hands on temples and then up, over and behind the ears, coming off the neck.*

Cross arms into the genie position, grasping a little higher [about an inch] up the arms this time.
Uncross and bring hands to Pharaoh, then Marilyn and then round to your back.

Trace down back of body and come off the side of the foot/little toe. Come up slowly, letting your abdominal girdle do the work. Maybe tracing a horizontal figure 8 with your arms as you come up.

My granny always said "never go upstairs empty handed", so I never just go up the body, I'll figure 8 or fluff my way up!

FLOWER ESSENCE SUPPORT

Flower and plants have been used since the beginning of time by healers of all cultures. Each contains a 'vibration', an energy. The essence captures that energy in a homeopathic liquid form.

They are particularly helpful in dealing with emotional

issues and are an effective addition to any of these above techniques.

They can be taken:–

- Directly into the mouth. Don't let the glass 'dropper' touch your mouth, as this could allow bacteria back into the bottle.

- Diluted in water and drunk. Use pure mineral water.

In addition, some can be:–

- Added to bath water
- Added to massage oil
- Applied directly to the skin (e.g. Slender Rice Flower over scar tissue)
- Mist with water in a fine mist spray. Spritz yourself or your home. E.g. Fringed Violet is excellent for clearing negative energies
- Added to the water to feed your plants or pets

The effects/benefits of taking an essence are normally subtle. Occasionally, they can be dramatic as your 'inner self' rushes to release unwanted, negative emotions and you feel the full force of them. Be assured however, flower essences can do no serious harm.

There are many essences available. The Australian Bush Flower Essences and Healing Herbs are my personal favourites. If you have difficulty finding them, contact the International Flower Essence Repertoire www.healingorchids.com which is an Aladdin's cave of essences from all around the world. Alternatively

Nutricentre in London do a great mail order service.

"The effect of these Essences is similar to that of meditation in that they enable the person to access the wisdom of their Higher Self. This releases negative beliefs held in the subconscious mind and allows the positive virtues of the Higher Self - love, joy, faith, courage etc. to flood their being. When this happens the negative beliefs and thoughts are dissolved, balance is restored and true healing occurs." IFER

Get advice or simply test to see which essences are the best for your current needs. Some of the Australian Bush Flower Essences that I have found particularly helpful are:–

BAUHINIA	*Where there is resistance to change, to new ideas*
BLACK EYED SUSAN	*THE stress essence !*
BLUEBELL	*For greed, fear of lack and emotional blocks*
FIVE COR-NERS	*To love yourself. Strengthens power of affirmations and stimulates flow of energy along the meridian pathways*
CROWEA	*For stress, worry and anxiety. Can 'seal in' the benefits of energy exercises.*
DOG ROSE	*Belief in self. Releasing fear and anxiety around the issue and new challenges.*

FRINGED VIOLET and STURT DESERT PEA	*Where the problem is associated with held-in emotional pain or trauma*
KAPOK BUSH	*Helps clarify the steps needed to achieve your goal. Gives confidence in your ability to succeed*
SUNSHINE WATTLE	*Creates a sense of optimism and hope*
ANGELSWORD	*One can read it as Angels word or Angel Sword but it is marvellous for cutting the cords that hold us tethered and prevents us reaching our full potential.*

'ASSEMBLING' IT ALL
Another optional extra

If your 'want' is profound, it may well touch your very soul. If it does, then it is worth working with an energy 'point' right in front of you.

The point is about the size of a tennis ball and is called The Assemblage Point and it sits about 2 feet in front of the centre of your chest.

It gathers, or 'assembles', information about your life experiences and processes them hand in hand with your very soul. It links your conscious and your soul. Around this sphere of energy your reality gathers.

"It sits in a band of light that encircles the body at the level of heart chakra, about two feet out from the chest in front of the body, and six to eight inches behind the body.

This band of light is formed from light that runs from the centre of the chest, coming out through heart chakra then spraying out in front of the chest like a cone. (This is called the "Hairs of Shiva in the Hindu tradition.)

The Assemblage Point is a sparkling, twinkling, alive energy that can look Tinkerbell-like".

Is how Donna Eden[20] describes the AP

Working with your wants you are trying to shift your reality and it pays to get your Assemblage point on board, it can bring calmness to both the heart and mind.

Get it balanced and in the right position and you literally walk towards what your soul 'knows', your destiny. It has the ability to call into your life anything that is needed: people, events, opportunities, thoughts etc.,

As you may have gathered this is powerful and profound work and should always be carried out with energy of love, gentleness and respect. There is an inherent wisdom in the AP that may not appear logical to our linear minds, so we never try and force the AP in any direction it isn't willing to go with.

Profound stresses in life can literally knock your AP off centre. You may not feel it at first but will begin to

20 Donna Eden. Eden Energy Medicine www.innersoure.net

notice that life doesn't flow smoothly, you feel slightly disconnected or disoriented in life, you literally are no longer walking towards your destiny.

I am not going to cover the really deep work that therapists can do with the AP, that would be irresponsible but I do offer you a very simple and safe technique to align your AP with your want. Bearing in mind, this is a spiritual point and won't do anything unless it is for your higher good!

Working with it will help you feel more hopeful and positive about achieving your 'want'; and once you start feeling that way you will begin to attract positivity into your life.

Rub your hands together and shake off excess energy.

I love to use Frankincense oil with this technique – simply rub some on your hands.

Hold the palms of your hands 2 feet away from and facing the centre of your chest. Breathe deeply and feel the energy between your hands and your chest.

Now Figure 8 in front of your chest – you are connecting to your AP. Imagine a horizontal '8' connecting to that tennis ball in front of you – about 2 feet away.

Smile and say – *"I walk towards my xyz [name want] in the most divine way – with love, all is well"*.

Do this about 10 times.

Hold the Spleen Neurovascular holding points – 2 inches above the top tip of each ear. Close your eyes and breathe deeply as Spleen energy helps your body metabolise this process.

Now hold the Heart Neurovascular holding point located right on the top of the head. Holding until you feel pulses in the top of your fingers as the blood floods into the point. Think of how it will be when you achieve your want, visualise it and being in all your senses. How would you feel if you had it right now?

Finally, take a cut glass prism ball, if you have one, and spin from the centre of your chest out to the AP and back again – repeat a few times.

Integrate the correction with a technique taken from Tibet that unscrambles the energies making for clearer communication, clearer thinking, improved left/right brain integration and cheers you up in no time at all, so great for when you are feeling sad, confused or angry. It returns your energy circuits to default, reduces stress, and encourages release of past emotional baggage or trauma. It sets a good, solid, calm support to achieve your wants.

- Bring your hands into prayer position in front of your chest, close your eyes and take a couple of breaths.

- Feet are crossed at the ankles.

- Put your arms out in front of you, palms facing outwards, as if you were doing breast stroke in the pool.

- Cross the wrists so your hands are palm to palm.

- Intertwine your fingers; pull them towards you, up 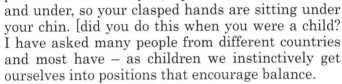 and under, so your clasped hands are sitting under your chin. [did you do this when you were a child? I have asked many people from different countries and most have – as children we instinctively get ourselves into positions that encourage balance.

- Keep your eyes closed, or look up at the sky, breath and smile. Hold for as long as you want – a minute?

Earlier on in the book I talked about correcting the meridians that tested weak, I gave you a list – here are the instructions. They are used to make the corrections and reprogramming and also make effective homework, along with tracing the weak meridians [explained earlier in the book or go on my site www.midlifegoddess.ning. com click onto the video section and there is a meridian tracing clip].

MERIDIAN CORRECTIONS IN DETAIL

Central	Empty out and zip up
Governing	Hook up
Stomach	Stomach 36 – the Master Point – 3 Mile Point
Spleen	Monkey thump
Heart	Massage Heart 8 [the genie in your hand] 9 Hearts with affirmation
Small Intestine	Pulse the source point
Bladder	Rub vigorously Bladder 1 – 3 several times
Kidney	K27
Circ Sex	Trace the pathway
Triple Warmer	Teddy Boy Sweep
Gallbladder	Massage GB20 – the Wind Pool
Liver	Rub the Neurolymphatic reflex points under the right breast
Lung	Rub Neurolymphatic reflex points them rake out to Lung 1 and 2 and massage firmly
Large Intestine	Massage firmly the outside of each thigh, where the seam of your trousers sits.

Place hands over your head, arms straight, fists clenched, wrists crossed.

Breathing out, bring hands down quickly and with force, un-crossing and taking them out to the side of the thighs with fingers now outstretched, not clenched.

While doing this, imagine a line that runs down the centre of the body, from mouth to the genital area. Imagine this line opening up, becoming 'unzipped' and any anger, rage, irritation, or negative energetic 'gunk' that has been lurking inside finally spilling out into the earth.

At the same time breathe out with a hissing sound and imagine all those angry toxic emotions, energies and thoughts spilling out on your breath.

Repeat 3 times

You are now 'open' and it is important to zip up that Central Meridian so that toxic energies that may be around you can no longer enter and cause disruption.

107

This zip up boosts confidence and positivity and clears your thoughts.

Simply place your hand at the bottom of the meridian [between your legs]. Take a deep in-breath and simultaneously move your hand up the centre of the body to your lower lip and 'lock it' by lightly tweaking the sides of your mouth.

As you do this, think of calmness, forgiveness and tranquillity around the whole issue of your want. A quiet certainty that you will achieve it with ease.

Do this 3 times and end by 'sewing up' i.e. tracing a horizontal Figure of 8 up the centre line, rather like an old fashioned Victorian corset.

Governing **The Classic Hook up.**

'Discombobulated'... I simply love the sound of this word although I have my doubts as to its 'official' existence, but just the sound of it manages to describe how we can all feel occasionally: Uncoordinated in both body and mind; a bit 'off'; a little 'spaced out'; stuck; not fully in the flow of life and unable to cope with the challenges life sets us.

Certainly not able to feel the clarity and focus required to work on getting our wants fulfilled.

This simple technique is a hyperlink to harmony and balance. It connects [hooks up] two important channels of energies: Governing and Central. It brings clarity of thought and purpose; strengthens the auric field and bridges the energies between the head and the body. You will feel less vulnerable more connected, co-ordinated, grounded and able to cope; your courage will be renewed as you head towards your want.

- Place the middle finger of one hand on your forehead between the eyebrows, over the 3rd Eye

- Place the middle finger of the other hand in your navel.

- With a slight pull of the skin upward on both points, close your eyes, take a deep breath and relax. [Breathe in through the nose and out through the mouth]

Stay in this position for about twenty seconds [or a few minutes, whatever feels right to you]. Eyes closed, deep breathing and don't forget to smile.

By strengthening the Governing Channel that runs up the back, you affect the spine, not only in a physical sense but also in an emotional way – literally giving you the 'backbone' to face and resolve problems and move forward in your life to achieve your want.

By strengthening the Central Channel that runs up the front of the torso you will be less vulnerable to absorbing other peoples' negative energies. An overdose of these can cause exhaustion and even depression; never a good emotional landscape for positive change.

> *It is a powerful tool for quickly centring yourself and has immediate neurological consequences.*

STOMACH   3 MILE POINT

This bend opens up the whole area around your middle [belt area] and creates space for energy to flow through all the organs in the mid torso and up the gallbladder and spleen meridians. It affects the extraordinary vessel called Belt Flow which increases your ability to balance being grounded and inspired. Between being happily off with the fairies and getting your drains fixed!

Holding Stomach 36 points gives you a burst of energy.

This acupoint is called the 3 Mile points and is one of acupunctures 'master points'.

Go to the knee, place your opposite palm around the leg with your index finger along the bottom edge of the kneecap the point will be under the 3rd or 4th finger – flex and point the foot to find the point in the muscle belly 2 fingers to the outside [lateral] of the centre of the shinbone... it will probably be tender

This is a very powerful and frequently used acupuncture point [I think of it as one point does all] that is particularly helpful for a number of imbalances in the abdominal region as well as strengthening the blood and the energy in the stomach meridian.

It is great for stable grounding in a mad world. Work these points when you feel tired yet need to carry to, it will revive you – but don't abuse it!

> There is a legend that says a general in an ancient Chinese army needed his troops to march more, but they were all exhausted from fighting and marching for so many weeks, they stopped and refused to go further. The general ordered his army doctor to stimulate St36 on every soldier – legend has it that the troops marched for another 3 miles and reached their destination – hence the point is called Three Mile Point.

Working with Stomach meridian is about self care, trusting in the mystery of life, trusting that your want will be fulfilled and letting go of unnecessary anxiety – relax and enjoy the ride, stop worrying – you can't change the past and who knows what tomorrow will bring – live fully grounded in the moment, that is one of the secrets of happiness.

- Stand with feet firmly on the ground, about hip width apart

- Bend your knees slightly and imagine yourself rooting down into the earth, feeling grounded and stable

- Close your eyes and place your palms on your thighs and take a couple of deep breaths and smile. Come into the present moment.

- Straighten up and bring your hands into prayer position in front of your chest, put a little pressure against your Thymus while you there – just 10 seconds.

- Take your right hand onto your right leg on the St 36 points, apply a little pressure.

- At the same time take your left arm up over your head and bend sideways. Make sure you are not tipping forward or backwards. Success is not how far over you go, it is feeling a good, painless stretch down the whole of your left side. [if you prefer, you can do this technique sitting in a chair].

- Stay in that position for 30 seconds

- Come back to centre and prayer position – press against the Thymus

- Repeat on the other side, again hold the pose for 30 seconds

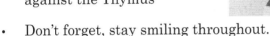

- Come back to centre and prayer position – press against the Thymus

- Don't forget, stay smiling throughout.

You could even say THANK YOU, in advance, for your 'want' materialising.

SPLEEN monkey thump

These are great little points to do every day. Not only will they help you process and deal with change, thus preparing the ground for your want, they will also:

- Boosts Immune System and general energy levels.
- Increases your ability to accept/metabolise changes.
- Balances blood chemistry.
- Aids detoxification of the body.
- Helps metabolise and absorb nutrients.
- Improves absorption of supplements [tap for 5 seconds before and after taking them].

You will be massaging/ tapping/thumping the 21st acupressure points on each Spleen meridian. These are located on the side of the ribcage, roughly where the bottom line of a bra would sit [see photo]. You will know when you hit on them as they will be tender.

Once located, you'll know when you are on the right point because if you dig in with your fingertips it will hurt. Use your clenched fists to massage, tap or thump firmly the points for a minimum of 5 seconds.

Breathe and smile.

HEART – 9 hearts

Stand tall, feel your roots in the earth beneath your feet, smile and take a few relaxing breaths.

Place the tips of your fingers [maybe with a little Frankincense, rose geranium or essential oil of your choice rubbed into the skin] on the area between your eyebrows.

Trace up over your eyebrows, down the side of your face to your chin, like tracing a heart on your face. Do 3 times.

Drop your fingertips to the bottom end of your breastbone and now trace 3 hearts over your torso: up over your breasts and down to the genital area.

Now place your fingers right on top of your head and trace 3 big hearts around your entire body; bringing your arms down slowly and deliberately, feel yourself moving the energies.

Bring your hands into prayer position against your chest, press in over the Thymus, them bring them up over your head and bring them down very slowly as you breath out.

This is very effective in stimulating the flow of the ancient 'Strangeflows' [Regulator is one of these] – they are the energies of joy and change.

SMALL INTESTINE – find the source

On the outside of the hand, in line with the little finger and just above the wrist – see diagram.

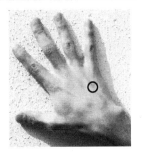

Hold it with your fingertips then trace small Figure 8s over the point.

Source Points are acupressure points where energy gathers on the meridians; they could be considered rather like 'holding tanks' for energy on each meridian.

Working with them sends concentrated energy from a meridian to an organ governed by that meridian. So they are a 'source' of energy, hence the name. If Small Intestine is strong it helps with all transformation, which is of course, what you are trying to achieve.

Think of how complex our world has become in the past fifty years – how much more difficult it has become to be discerning and discriminating. Choice has become constant in our lives in all aspects from what to watch on TV tonight, between different foodstuffs, drinks, jobs, holidays, to getting married or getting a mortgage. Just imagine what a strain that is on your Small Intestine.

If our ability to separate the pure from the impure becomes weakened, we can become confused or indecisive and can struggle to even see clearly what choices are available. The pros and cons just swirl around in your mind. You enter a panicked indecision. Sound familiar?

BLADDER
Forehead rubbing.

I really love this quick technique. It only takes ten seconds, how's that for fast results? Take the middle fingers of each hand and place the pads gently on the inside edge of the eye socket, get on the bone, increase the pressure and push up towards hairline. Repeat vigorously about ten times. You are stimulating the first points on the Bladder meridian.

I have also found that by doing this, you can help prevent an epileptic fit. But it has to be immediately the person feels 'an aura' – keep doing for 20-30 seconds, breathing deeply.

KIDNEY – K27 points

One of the real energy medicine staples, massaging these points ensures your energies are running in the right direction. A fundamental need for optimum energy function. It also:

- Jump-starts and energises the entire system.
- Balances disruptions caused by travelling, especially through time zones. [A great one to do during a flight and when you step off the plane].
- Brings clarity to thought
- Improves focus and concentration.
- Brings a flow back into your life.
- Temporarily energises the eyes, useful if you are tired but still have a few more miles to drive.

You will be tapping and therefore stimulating the 27th acupuncture point on each Kidney meridian. These important points act as 'junction boxes' for other meridians.

They are located near the 'right angle' where the collar and breast bones meet. You will feel two natural indentations that may be slightly tender when you press them.

Don't worry if you can't find the exact points, you know the approximate area, so tap around and you will get them, as with all energy work, it is about intention and attention.

Breathe, fully moving your rib cage and diaphragm. Smile and tap for 5 seconds.

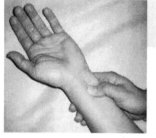

CIRCULATION SEX – a true master point

The 6th point on this meridian.

About 2 inches below the wrist crease in line with the middle finger. Called the INNER GATE - this is an amazing point for calming the mind, **insomnia**, anxiety, irritability, emotional upset, crying, mood swings and depression. It does so much I can't help but think of it as a **master point** par excellence!

My favourite technique is to stroke, circle or figure 8 it gently with your fingertips – in whatever direction feels right.

This point responds really well to essences/oils/crystals being placed on it – lavender or rose geranium for example.

It is particularly useful if your 'want' is associated with a relationship issue.

This 'inner gate' can be thought of as opening and closing to allow others into our hearts. When we experience constant 'heart ache/break' and disappointment in 'love' and close relationships our inner gate can close firmly; not wanting to allow any more pain into the energy field.

However, by closing this gate you also trap in all that old pain.

We have to have the courage to open our inner door so old pain can leave, we can heal and we can embrace life with an 'open heart' – this is the only way to spiritual development and achieving our wants.

Yes, you may indeed get hurt again, growth is through experience of this kind and it also teaches us the valuable lesson of 'discernment' [not necessarily judgement, but the wisdom of discernment]. In this way we, and our relationships, can blossom.

TRIPLE WARMER – Teddy Boy Sweep

You will be aligning the energy of your hands with the end of the meridian, on each temple. Once aligned you trace backwards along part of the pathway. Working in this direction, calms and sedates the energy around your want issue.

Place the palms of each hand against each temple.

Take a deep breath in and as you breathe out trace the hands up the front of the ear, over the top and down behind the ear.

Down the neck to the point where a necklace would naturally fall, pull off firmly along that necklace line and end by shaking off both hands.

Do this a couple of times and you will instantly feel calmer. In fact as a species, many of us, irrelevant of culture, automatically do the beginning part of the Teddy Boy Sweep when we feel overwhelmed or stressed in any way.

GALLBLADDER – massage the Wind Pool

Place your thumbs on your earlobes. Slide them back toward the centre of your neck. Now your thumbs will be approximately one thumb width above the hairline of your neck. Your thumbs will fall into a depression on either side of the vertebra of your neck, at the base of the skull. (If you slowly bend your head forward and then back again, you will be able to identify these depressions easily.)

The points called 'Wind Pool' is located in these depressions.

A good way to work GB20 is to have your friend lie down, with no cushion under the head. Curl the tips of your fingers under the occipital bone [skull] and lift and pull firmly to open the area and let the weight of the head rest upon your fingers. This perpendicular pressure is very powerful – you can also massage if you prefer. Self massage is very easy with your thumbs.

They are master points at calming the mind and relaxing the body. They will help you gain the flexibility to make the changes necessary changes to gain your want.

LIVER – under the boob

A quick way to bring balance to the Liver meridian is to massage, very firmly underneath your right boob, exactly where the underwire of a bra sits. There are points called Neurolymphatic and are reflex points directly to the organ. They may be tender but don't let up on the pressure, keep it firm, the soreness is simply a sign you need it.

LUNG – get the point

Locate the first two points on the lung meridian. The easiest way to find this area is don't think too much about it, bring your elbow to your side and throw your arm up to the area on the opposite shoulder, normally where the middle finger lands is the area you need to massage or figure 8 – you may find it is tender to the touch, so pressure should be firm but not too painful, be careful if working with someone who is fragile ... less is sometimes more.

Working these points also helps any shoulder and chest problems, loosen up. It increases the flow of energy to the lungs and so is important for all respiratory disorders, especially coughing and difficulty in breathing.

If you are stuck, exhausted, sluggish, depressed or despondent or holding onto emotional pain – Lung 1 can help you regain a joy in life and uplift you renewing your optimism about achieving your want.

Breathe deeply as you work the point. Sometimes when you hold these points, you will find the tears come, let them, they need to exit your body so you can recover and move on.

If you find anything too distressing, keep it in your mind and hold the forehead holding points while it passes through you.

I call these two points the Oh My God points as they are situated exactly where you would place your hand on your forehead when stressed. Halfway between your eyebrow and hairline in line with your eyes when they are looking straight ahead, these two points are your new best friends. Hold them with fingertips until you feel a pulse. This signals that the blood is moving from the back to the forebrain.

Excellent when problems seem insurmountable; when you are so deeply caught up in grief or concern; when a child is fearful after a nightmare.

Hold the back of your skull for extra reassurance.

LARGE INTESTINE – the trouser line

Massage firmly up and down the outside of each thigh, exactly where the seam of your trousers sits. Again, you will be working Neurolymphatic points, so they may be a bit tender but persist.

With any of the above corrections remember to smile, breathe and even say your affirmation as you do them.

SOME MORE OPTIONAL EXTRAS

This is an excellent piece of advice that I received a few months ago – so obvious and so effective and huge fun to implement.

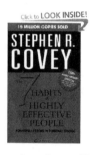

Click to LOOK INSIDE!
15 MILLION COPIES SOLD
STEPHEN R. COVEY
7 HABITS HIGHLY EFFECTIVE PEOPLE

Take time to sharpen your saw.

In his book, The 7 Habits of Highly Effective People, Stephen Covey calls the seventh habit, "Sharpen the Saw." Essentially, this means pausing from production efforts and giving yourself an opportunity to experience personal renewal in one or more of the four key dimensions of your life: Physical, mental, social-emotional, and spiritual.

To illustrate this principle, Covey tells about a man strolling through the woods when he hears a sawing noise. Investigating, the nature-lover sees a man perspiring profusely as he attempts to cut down a large tree.

"What are you doing?" the observer asks. "I'm cutting down this tree, can't you see?" is the response.

"No, I mean, it looks like you have been working hard. How long have you been doing this?" "Two hours." "Why don't you take some time to sharpen the saw? It will make things go much faster and easier." "I don't have time to do that – I have to get this tree cut down!"

Balance your root chakra

As I said at the beginning, the basic technique can be used with other energy systems. For example the Chakra system.

Here I am just going to offer you an exercise to gently bring the root chakra back into balance – this relates very closely to Maslow's pyramid [the lowest rung].

It sits over the coccyx/genital area – the lowest rung on the torso.

It is about our basic, rational survival needs, about grounding, security, self preservation, safety and tribal belonging. It also houses our ancestral memories and our animal instinct that can alert us to danger. In contemporary life: survival, security and safety equates more with money, career, pensions and housing rather than hunting for meat and bringing it back to the tribe. If you fear not being able to pay the mortgage and bills, this chakra will begin to shrink and you begin to enter a downward energetic spiral.

So, you can appreciate how important it is to keep your root chakra in good shape.

One very simple way is to simply **'stir the soup'**

Imagine a clock face sitting over the chakra area.

With your hand just away from the body, so not actually touching it, take a moment to connect in with the area.

Slowly start circling your left hand [or both hands if you prefer] in an anti-clockwise [*hence imagining the clock to help you find the right direction*] circle above the chakra.

Feel the energy, where is it? What is it doing? Your hand is acting like a magnet and drawing out toxic/stagnant energy from the chakra. Keep circling until you feel a change in the energy. Visualise the energy coming up and out of the chakra.

Take time and focus: how do you feel? do you have any thoughts or pictures coming into your mind that might be relevant?

Shake off your hands onto the floor, so the earth can take up the energy and transmute it.

Now circle your other hand [right or both] in a clockwise direction above the same chakra. This will harmonise the energy. Keep circling until you feel the energy is strong. Take as long as you need. Concentrate and remember to breathe.

End by tracing a figure 8, in whatever direction you choose, over the area.

You might like to tape a little frankincense resin somewhere on the area or rub essential oil in your hands before you do the balancing.

> Another way, slightly more complicated is to sedate a meridian called Circulation Sex, the muscles associated with this meridian are located in the root chakra, so sedating the energy, empties out stagnant old energy and allows new energy to come flooding in and, of course, flow; that in turn affects [positively] the root chakra.

Simply hold the first set of points until you feel a pulse and then the second set, again until you feel a pulse.[21]

Repeat on the other side of the body.

---

21 With grateful thanks to Donna Eden for sharing her illustration of the points. Suggested reading is her book Energy Medicine.

Another fun way to boost this energy is to dance. Try belly dancing, moving the whole pelvic area will stimulate the energy.

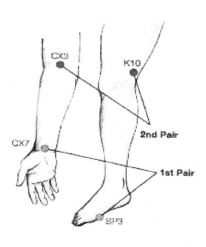

Sedating Points

Whatever you do in life, but especially if you are a healer or therapist of any kind, it is vital to be grounded fully with Earth, to be in the present. We all have our own methods for grounding – for example my Coming to Your Senses [below] exercise is perfect. However, let me introduce you to another grounding exercise that you may like to try:

If you can do this outdoors, in the country, by the sea, perhaps with your spine against a favourite tree – it enhances the technique.

- Sit or stand – whatever is comfortable for you. Take some deep breaths, really open up your lungs.

- Visualise yourself as a tree, a strong tree, reaching up the sky with your leaves and your roots burrowing down deeply into Mother Earth. Feel the sun warming your skin/bark and the air against your face.

- BREATHE IN from the sky, sun and air; feel the breath running down through your body, like a waterfall, cleansing every particle of you.

- BREATHE OUT, down through your feet/roots and let any negativity flow out of you, in the earth which can take whatever negativity your throw at it and transmute it positively.

- BREATHE IN through your feet/roots – deeply. Feel the nurturing, healing energy of Mother Earth surge up through your body, replenishing you, feeding you.

- BREATHE OUT and feel all tension leaving your body, creating space for energy to flow.

Repeat this two or three times until you feel calm, grounded, cleansed and replenished.

- Now take a few moments to visualise your roots deep down in the earth, spread out, holding you to this planet, they are strong, they are your support, your connection... feel them.

- Say a prayer, ask for protection, for strength, for balance, for renewed health: for whatever you feel you need and don't forget to say 'thank you' in advance.

- Be still for a minute and if you feel 'good' – programme that feeling into your body by gently tapping your 3rd eye.

CUTTING CORDS!

If a chakra is resistant to balancing, there may be a cord getting in the way.

Often we develop etheric cords on individual chakras. They will attach to the chakra and draw energy from it. One of the most common cords is a sexual one to the lower chakras, they can stay in place for up to 7 years after an affair is finished, before they begin to dissolve.

They can attach to different chakras. For example:

- Feet – holding us to where we live, home, geographic locations [not so good if you are trying to sell your house!]
- Root and Womb – sexual/lovers/tribe [need to cut with the past if your 'want' involves a new partner
- Solar Plexus – conflicts that have impact – ego and fear holding you back?
- Heart – grief – feel, honour and let move through
- Throat – unresolved communication.

Cord cutting does not mean anything other than letting go of the dysfunctional part of a relationship/memory. More often than not this is fuelled by a fear of some kind.

Hold the intention of letting go [with love] of the cords that block you feeling joy and experiencing positive change in your life.

Mentally take hold of the cord, identify it, call it's attention, thank it for the lesson it has been instrumental in teaching you, tell it that it is now time to let go and move on, take your sacred dagger, sword or scissors and slowly cut the cord, releasing fear, forgiving the person/situation and letting go of any attachment. Smile and feel the peace of this moment. Focus on any little bit of cord still attached and see it disintegrate and fresh new energetic skin growing over.

You are free to move on.

Letting go on a breath

This exercise stimulates the neurolymphatic points relating to the Lung and Large Intestine [letting go] and draws on the power of visualisation to release negative elements [and people] from your life enabling you to move on.

- Firmly massage down the breastbone
- Move fingers to either side of the bone and massage firmly upwards
- Repeat 3 times

- Firmly massage down the outside of the thigh [where the trouser seam sits], in a straight line from top of thigh to just above the knee. You can do both thighs at the same time.
- Repeat 3 times

- Take a deep breath and relax
- Bring to mind the person, situation, negative

element or emotion you want to release from your life. What is it that is blocking you from getting your 'want'?

- Exhale and imagine you are blowing him/her/it out of your inner depths
- Repeat 3 times

Now for the extra piece of magic ...

- Cup hands together in front of chest/neck area and imagine the person, situation, or representation of the emotion sitting there in your hands – about the size of a chess piece

- Inhale deeply and as you very slowly exhale, visualise him/her/it being blown away, scattering into the wind and disappearing into the distant horizon.[22] At the same time thinking *"xyz leave my life, in love and in the most divine way – GOODBYE, go in peace"*

- Take a couple of deep breaths and smile.

- Try ending with the exercise empty out and zip up [below]

I was shown this technique on the Island of Gozo, on the cliffs overlooking the sea – a perfect location to let go of negativity, send it back to the earth [her ability to take the negative and transform it]and water [cleansing/ new beginnings]. I often do it now with people who I find too aggressive, competitive, negative or generally depleting!

---

22 Needless to say, this is not an exercise to be done in front of your mirror!

So it you want to end with **empty out and zip up** – this is how you do it. It will remove any last residue of that person/thing/energy that you are trying to let go on a breath.

Stand tall, close your eyes and take some deep breaths, really expanding the ribcage. This in itself begins the balancing process.

Place hands over your head, arms straight, fists clenched, wrists crossed.

Breathing out, bring hands down quickly and with force, uncrossing and taking them out to the side of the thighs with fingers now outstretched, not clenched.

While doing this, imagine a line that runs down the centre of the body, from mouth to the genital area. Imagine this line opening up, becoming 'unzipped' and any anger, rage, irritation, or negative energetic 'gunk' that has been lurking inside finally spilling out into the earth... certainly any residue of whatever it is you have been trying to let go off on your breath – there could be a sneaky little bit left clinging energetically to you, this will get rid of it.

At the same time breathe out with a hissing sound and imagine all those angry toxic emotions, energies and thoughts spilling out on your breath.

Repeat 3 times

You are now 'open' and it is important to zip up that Central Meridian so that toxic energies that may be around you can no longer enter and cause disruption. This zip up boosts confidence and positivity and clears your thoughts.

Simply place your hand at the bottom of the meridian [between your legs]. Take a deep in-breath and simultaneously move your hand up the centre of the body to your lower lip and 'lock it' by lightly tweaking the sides of your mouth.

As you do this, think of calmness, forgiveness and tranquillity being zipped up inside

Do this 3 times and end by 'sewing up' i.e. tracing a horizontal Figure of 8 up the centre line, rather like an old fashioned Victorian corset.

This will give you a wonderful protection against external energies entering your body; against some of the stresses of life triggering unnecessary anger. It does not stifle you; you can still give out care, warmth, attention and love.

Coming to your senses

This is a gently effective technique that brings you easily into a state of calmness that is ideal to do:

- before or after your 'Daily Energy Exercises or

- by itself whenever you feel drawn to it or

- forthesheerjoyofexperiencingthetranquillityitbrings.

- when you visit a new place – mountains, sea, building etc., and seek to connect to that place.

- when you need to get off the merry go round and still the chatter of the daily grind

- ifyouareapersonwhoisdriventobe'doing'something all the time and finds it hard to sit and smell the roses!

First things first...

When did you last take time to smell the flowers? I have to say that when I am in Andalucía, it is very easy to sit quietly and just 'be' and that is one of the reasons I am so often here.

However, I remember when I was in London, I would find myself rushing around, busily getting things done to keep pace with the urban fixation on 'speed'. My mind could easily become 'clenched' and rigid, filled with useless thoughts, concerns, unfounded anxieties, lists, lists about lists and endless planning.

I lost touch with that still/peaceful place inside myself. I became like the White Rabbit in Wonderland! Occasionally, even nowadays a whisper of that stressful clenching can appear in my life, my rabbit pops out of her burrow and the days get shorter and my action list gets longer and time shrinks and I begin to think of organizing my life in 30 minute segments – I know then it is time to COME TO MY SENSES

One of the basic principles of EM is FLOW and

nothing whatsoever is going to flow through a clenched mind!

How do you 'de-clench'? Any technique that relaxes and frees the mind will work: meditation, prayer, exercise, yoga – the list is endless.

If you are confused and not sure what to do, try this simple technique to exercise your senses. It will gently slow down and stop the merry-go-round, bringing you into the peaceful clarity of the 'here and now'.

It is a great technique for bringing you into the present. Rather than trying deliberately to empty your mind of all the thoughts that plague and pester you, by giving your mind something else to focus on, those thoughts automatically disappear. If they creep back, and they will every few seconds/minutes, don't fight them, just return your attention to the 'sense' you are working. You cannot move forward smoothly in life if you are tethered by the minutiae of small thoughts, each one acting like a guy rope holding you down and preventing you flowing with the natural rhythm of your life.

I can hear some of you saying: *'that's all well and good for her, but I don't have TIME to do this or any other technique'* – Don't you?

Then life is ruling you rather than you living your life.

Look at your schedule carefully, with inspection you will find the time by cutting out something that is not constructive: a little less TV, getting up a little earlier, going to bed a little later, taking a shorter lunch break, a little less talking on the phone ... Think! You can find a few minutes a day for yourself. It will be the best investment of time you will ever make.

Coming to Spain really opened my eyes to how much time I 'wasted' in the UK. When I arrived, with no landline, no easy computer access, no English television, no shops nearby to tempt me, no nearby friends to see or call, suddenly I found myself with hours of extra 'time'. It is amazing how much time we fritter away.

Okay, so how do you do it?[23]

Find a quiet corner in your home or go for a walk in nature and pick a safe, peaceful place to sit.

---

23 Timings are approximate: you can stay with each sense for a minute or ten minutes – experiment to see what suits you.

Ideally sit in the Lotus pose, but if this is not possible for you, find a comfortable position where your spine is straight. A straight spine is vital so that energy can more freely flow up and down the spinal column and therefore out to the entire body.

Once you are comfortable, take a few deep breaths and do the **Teddy Boy Sweep** [see description on page 120] to calm down the Triple Warmer energy.

1. Now close your eyes and just focus on what you can **HEAR** – keep your breathing natural. Peel back the layers of what is going on around you and you will be astonished at what you start to hear. Remain with this for 2 minutes and if distracting thoughts come into your head don't worry, just gently take yourself back to the sense of 'hearing'.

2. Keeping your eyes closed, focus on what you can **SMELL**[24] for a few minutes

3. Still with eyes closed, **TOUCH**[25] something. Again, 2 minutes.

4. Focus, for a couple of minutes, on something in front of you and really **SEE** it.

5. If you are outdoors, **'FEEL'** how the environment

---

24 You might like to prepare some items to touch or smell. For example a flower, an essential oil, a herb, a sprig of mint

25 You can simply touch your hair, nail, skin, grass, sand or whatever is around you OR be prepared and take along a tumbled crystal, a feather, a leaf – something deliciously tactile, a piece of lavender to smell.

touches you: feel the breeze in your hair, the sun on your skin, or the rain on your face... Bring ALL your attention to the sensations.

6. Bring your focus to your body, mentally run up it from your toes to the crown of your head and **FEEL** each and every part of it. This is not easy and sometimes when I do it I can't 'feel' a thing, if this happens to you, just remain with it, sooner or later you will begin to 'feel', begin to reconnect with every cell in your body.

This reconnection is vital for our health and wellbeing. All too often we live in our heads and disconnect with our bodies, an alienation that can ultimately disrupt every system.

When you have mastered this 'feeling', take it a step further and isolate a particular part of your body and focus your sense of 'feeling' on it. I personally isolate my spine. Leaning forward slightly in the lotus position, to stretch it. I use my mind and feel along it vertebrae by vertebrae, really experiencing the sensations. If there is stiffness or pain, after a while it will begin to diminish and release. Don't forget your breathing, which should be natural and flowing.

Optional ending

Sit on your heels, or in lotus position or in a chair – whatever is comfortable to you.

Put your arms behind you and clasp your left wrist with your right hand and make a circle with your finger and thumb [left hand].

Lean forward as far as you can. Stay comfortable, going a little bit further with each out breath.

This pose is deeply relaxing and balancing in the sense that it encourages the release of deep seated emotional baggage.

Come out of the pose slowly and sit quietly, perhaps saying your personal prayer or read an inspirational quote and ponder upon it.

Use this as an opportunity for a minute or two of quiet contemplation and cultivating your attitude of gratitude.

Another benefit of coming to your senses is that by putting them through their paces they improve and ultimately, it may take a long time, once they reach optimum efficiency the other more esoteric senses begin to develop and emerge into the open.

Summary

So you've read the book, maybe been to a workshop or watched the video clips. You've gained knowledge about how to remove the blocks that are stopping you living the life you have always wanted; enjoying money and realising your wants.

However there is a catch!

You have to do your daily Wealth Workout.

Make a commitment to do it for the next month, it will only take a couple of minutes every day. You will then begin to notice things changing. It may be slow at first but they will change. Once you actually see it work you will be totally hooked!!

I know it seems that there is a lot to do but once you get the hang of it, it is so quick and easy. So chin up and persevere for the first couple of days as you get used to your Wealth Workout.

Let me summarise the basic protocol. As always, if you get stuck, if I haven't explained something clearly enough, just email me; I am here to help you achieve your want – you are not alone.

Preparation	Take time out to decide and clearly define what it is you 'want'. There may be many things, identify the priority 'want' at the moment, maybe write it down.
	Make use of Mudra on Forehead and Genie in your hand techniques to help you gain some clarity.
Money	This is normally the key stumbling block
	Test to see what your core belief about money is.
Your want	Test your 'want' and note result to use later
Meridians And Money	Test money against each meridian
	Consider meaning of any weaknesses that emerge
	Correct weak meridians
	Retest
	Allocate homework

		IF STRONG
		Do homework [above] as the money issue was probably the only thing holding you back.
Further techniques to address your money 'issue' or your 'want'.	Retest it	
		IF WEAK
		Do you 'deserve' having more money/your want?
	Test on 'deserve' – do you think you are worth it?	**IF STRONG**
		'deserve' is not an issue so move onto safety issue
		IF WEAK
		Correct and retest
	Test on 'safety' – does your 'mini-me' feel it is safe for you?	**IF STRONG**
		Safety is not an issue. Move on to next stage
		IF WEAK
		Correct and retest

If you still weak – this block will need some deeper work.

Test for a psychological reversal and then the priority fear feeding it.

Reprogramme holding FHP + tapping ST3 + TW sedation points. Trace Regulator Flow.

Retest.

Compile your Daily Wealth Workout plan

After all this it should now test strong on money and your 'want'. There is nothing standing between you and your dreams!

Optional extras for you to consider trying

Temple tapping *[to turbo charge your affirmations]*	**Flower essence support** **Prosperity tips** *[for the sheer fun of it]*	**Assemblage Point** work Balance your **root chakra**
Clutter clearing *[create space in your life for the new to come in]*	**Read inspirational books**, *one of my biggest inspirations has been Stuart Wilde – he's written many books – visit his site:* *www.stuartwilde. com*	**Letting go** on a breath Coming to your senses

MADISON KING
writer and teacher of energy medicine

Madison's Medicine is a unique fusion of energy and body work, flower essences, lifestyle advice and commonsense — providing essential, everyday, practical tools for a healthier and happier you.

Many moons ago Madison was involved in the heart of London advertising, becoming a successful international board director. However, she realised, after a few ambition fuelled years, that she wanted her life to take a different direction and shocked everyone by giving up the BMW, Armani suits and Gucci briefcase, becoming a student again.

She trained in massage, sports massage, aromatherapy, Indian head massage, reflexology, trager, nutrition, flower essences, crystals, radionics ... A true workshop groupie, she filled a wall with qualifications but could not find what she had been seeking; she couldn't even really define it ... until, through divine synchronicity, she met Donna Eden in London through a mutual friend. Within no time at all she was in Ashland in Donna's backyard with about four other students, eagerly learning about energy – this was more than two decades ago, so no information highway was available in those days and ever the thirsty student she drank in everything she could on these visits, rushing back to London to experiment on her long suffering clients!

145

Over the years she crossed the ocean many times learning from Donna and also John Thie [Touch for Health].

She then began to teach Donna's work in the UK, USA, Gozo, Malta, Italy, Egypt and many other locations around the world, she has appeared on national television, radio and press promoting EEM. She has lectured at Westminster and Oxford universities and at the key Mind Body Spirit Festivals in London and Wales.

In 2006 she gave up a thriving practice in Central London and now divides her time between the Isle of Wight and the Andalucían town of Nerja in Southern Spain.

Just about to enter her 7th decade, she has set up and is running Donna Eden's training in Europe – based just outside London... a long way from those days in Donna's back yard!

Her focus is on promoting Donna's work in Europe and also writing and teaching her own version: Madison's Medicine, which based on Eden Energy Medicine and weaving in many other natural health threads, giving people simple yet powerful tools to enhance their quality of life on every single level.

Madison King
www.madisonking.com
www.midlifegoddess.ning.com
madisonking@hotmail.com
Facebook page: Madison's Medicine